FATIMA

Fatima Whitbread, Olympian and world javelin champion, is one of Britain's most famous and popular athletes. She lives in Essex.

Adrianne Blue, who has worked with Fatima Whitbread on the book, is an American living in London. She is a sports correspondent for *The Sunday Times*. Her previous books include *Grace under Pressure* and *Faster, Higher, Further: Women's Triumphs and Disasters at the Olympics*.

W9-BBY-003

Fatima

THE AUTOBIOGRAPHY OF
FATIMA WHITBREAD

with
ADRIANNE BLUE

SPHERE BOOKS LIMITED

A SPHERE BOOK

First published in Great Britain by Pelham Books, 1988
Published by Sphere Books Ltd, 1989

Printed and bound in Great Britain by
Cox & Wyman Ltd, Reading

Sphere Books Ltd
A Division of
Macdonald & Co (Publishers) Ltd
66–73 Shoe Lane
London EC4P 4AB
A member of Maxwell Pergamon Publishing Corporation plc

For Mum, Dad, Gregg and Kirk
and those very special people

To Daniel

Keep Smiling !

[signature]

xxx

Contents

Acknowledgements

This is a very personal book. Even so, it could not have been written without the assistance of the many people who gave freely and generously of their time and knowledge. I want to say thank you to Cory Boswell, Edna Dennis, Caradoc King, Andy Norman, Rae Peat, Alma Riley, Grandad and Nan, my brothers Gregg and Kirk, and Mum and Dad.

My warm thanks, too, to Adrianne Blue for helping me probe into the often painful past, and for making the manuscript a reality. In a few instances we have omitted or changed a name to avoid embarrassing anyone.

My thanks also to my publishers, Roger Houghton and Hilary Foakes, for guiding the book through to publication.

Above all I would like to thank the public who I have always found to be an inspirational help.

Fatima

1

Touch and Go

The worst moment of my life happened very early on. I was much too young to have any memory of it, but what I have always been told is this.

It was springtime in London, 1961. The sixties had not started properly swinging yet. It would be four years before the Beatles queued up to get their MBE. Reality for most British people was fish and chips only on Friday night and making ends meet.

In a council flat in North London – in the sort of drab, uninspired block about which I can well imagine Prince Charles being scathing – a baby began to cry.

The baby cried and cried and cried. For the next two or three days – it is unlikely to have been longer because a baby that young left unattended would not have lived any longer – the neighbours resisted ringing the police. Then someone in one of those flats picked up the telephone and dialled the Old Bill.

A three-month old baby was found lying in tangled sheets. The baby had been left alone in the empty flat with nothing to eat or drink. She was dehydrated, she was filthy, she was ill. That baby was me. I am told I could have died. And that if it had been colder I would have.

I like to think that whoever it was that should have been looking after me had just popped out for a quarter of an hour, which unexpectedly stretched into an hour and then days. Anyone could be forgiven for wanting to get away from that dingy block in Matthias Road, from the sweet, cloying scent of urine in the corridors, the crude graffiti on the walls. I want to believe that I was left unattended out of simple carelessness, not wickedness. I

1

want to believe that I was not, as Cory was later told, 'dumped'. I want to believe it was a sin of omission rather than commission.

The evidence suggests that the woman who gave birth to me never wanted me. She was a Cypriot with dark eyes and dark, wavy hair very like my own, but I do not regard her as my mother, and I am certain that as long as I live I never will. When I was born on 3 March 1961, in Bearsted Memorial Hospital in Stoke Newington, she neglected to register my birth. It was finally registered on 17 June 1961, after I had been found, when one of the social workers noticed the oversight. The birth certificate, which was not issued until three years later, on 20 July 1964, gives Adem as my father's name, but that is an error, perhaps even a joke.

I can imagine the woman who gave birth to me sitting in a DHSS office, or in the incredibly dirty kitchen I was made to scrub so many years later, telling an inquisitive social worker in broken English, 'The only man I know is Adem.' What the social worker would not have understood was that Adem was her three-year-old son.

At the time I was abandoned, Adem was either with his mother or perhaps it was one of the many periods when he was in care. As far as I can make out, his was not an idyllic childhood either. But Adem did live with her long enough, often enough, intimately enough, to learn to speak the language she spoke most easily, Cypriot. He saw her throughout his childhood, he did little errands for her, he ate the meals that she cooked for him. Such as she was, he had a mother. I did not.

The man who sowed the seed that created me was called Michael. He too was a Londoner and a Cypriot. I no more regard him as my father than I regard her as my mother.

My mother and father are Margaret and John Whitbread. But I was not to meet them until many years later, and when I did they transformed my life in every way. Not only did they give me a home and real family love – not only did they give me a new life – but they set me on course to becoming a champion.

I feel I must tell the story from the beginning. All of it. The high points – winning, shattering the world record, going to

2

Buckingham Palace for my own MBE two decades after the Beatles got theirs. And the heartbreak. At first, there was mainly heartbreak.

Suffering from severe malnutrition and neglect, I was rushed from the flat in North London to a children's hospital. There I was to spend my second three months. A GP has told me that few infants have survived so long on their own without water. If you look at it that way, I was, I suppose, rather lucky.

Apparently, the woman who gave birth to me told the authorities she was willing to have me back. But they felt she was inadequate, unable to look after me. On 23 November 1962 a Fit Person Order made the Council of the London Borough of Islington my legal guardians. I was made a ward of the court, in the care of the social services, who themselves, at first, seemed uncertain as to what to do with me. I was housed at no less than four homes as a baby.

At last, when I was three years old, a placement of sorts was made. It was now 1964, and the Beatles' song *Can't Buy Me Love* was on more than a million lips. I was moved from the swinging London of fast music, short mini-skirts and long puffs of marijuana, to Hertfordshire and the green and quiet countryside. This was the best thing that could possibly have happened to me, but it was not without grave difficulties.

2

The Yellow Brick House

They say you can't go home again, that it's never the same, but I went anyway — if you can rightly call that big, drafty, rambling house in Hertfordshire, where I spent the next two years of my life, home. To find out if Wormley Hill House on the outskirts of Greater London ever had been home, and to take a good, long look at it after so many years away, I drove up the A10 after breakfast one Wednesday afternoon, and pulled into the driveway.

The house, which has new owners now, was in the early stages of being done up. Building materials were strewn in the gravel drive, large beams lay in a heap just missing the front flowerbed, and looking through the groundfloor bay window into the room which had been my playroom, I could see that partitions had been hacked away. Although there was plenty of evidence of industry, there were no workmen about. Nor did anyone seem to be living there. A front window was open, and I climbed through.

Decades of paint and paper had been stripped from the walls preparatory to decorating, and the walls of the playroom which I shared with eight other children were no longer that calming pale blue. In all, there had been more than twenty of us at Wormley, scribbling pictures and fitting together our jigsaw puzzles in adjacent playrooms. Now the house was entirely empty and the planked wooden floors were caked with builders' dust. The kitchen was derelict, and the high ceilings and that long, steep, winding staircase where I used to cause as much fuss as possible, were in an even sorrier state than when I lived there.

But Wormley Hill House was, and is, a very impressive building. Standing in large grounds at a fork in the road which leads

4

from the village of Wormley Hill past the church into the green countryside, the house, with its grimy yellow brick and square, heavy architecture, could easily have been mistaken, even during the two lonely years I lived there, for a dilapidated country seat.

There certainly was nothing posh about us – the children from the home – but the house was gruesomely elegant, the towering ceilings needing only a glittering chandelier.

On my return, the staircase seemed less steep and a little less imposing than I recalled. That staircase, which still had the finger marks of little children on the white paintwork of the banister, brought back vivid memories of mornings at Wormley Hill.

The mornings were when Cory, a skinny sixteen-year-old and the person I cared most about in all the world, had very little time for me, none at all to give me any special attention. Not that the rest of her day was a doddle either – she woke us promptly at six a.m., she fed us, she amused us all day long, she bathed us, and when it was necessary because one of us was sobbing, she rocked us to sleep. But in the mornings she was busiest, getting all of us up, washed, dressed and fed, and delivering a few of us to the school bus.

Cory Kathleen Muddle, the youngest assistant at the home, had charge of the largest group of children, nine of us. Still a growing girl of under five foot, she had not yet noticed that she had a *haut couture* figure hidden under her loose, sensible, cotton dresses and those aprons with lumpy pockets bulging with crayons and knitting wool and little bags of sweets for us. Cory had steady blue eyes and a girlish, high-pitched voice, which despite its youthfulness, reassured me inside. Her expression of love for me felt as if it came from a tender heart, not professionalism.

Indeed, for as long as she could remember, Cory had wanted to care for children. While other girls went out to discos after school or studied for O levels, Cory sat at home reading books on childcare. It was only occasionally that she had time to watch her favourite pop star, Cliff Richard, on television.

Recommended by a sympathetic headmistress, she had left school specially to take this job, for which she was paid £2. 10s. 0d. a week. Even in those days, the salary was a pittance, a joke among her friends, most of whom earned at least £10 a week at their first jobs and who worked shorter and less emotional hours. But they were often bored at their jobs. Cory loved hers, perhaps too much, often fretting, even on the weekends that she was off duty and at home with her family, about what would become of us.

Because she had taken over from an experienced nurse who was highly qualified, Cory had gone in at the deep end, with her nine charges, including two babies in cots, a handful of children between four and six, and even one boy aged nine who was allowed to stay on long past the cut-off age of five because his younger sister was living there. When Cory arrived I was three and a half, a chunky, dark-haired little girl, with a will of iron. Or maybe it was a whim of iron. Thank goodness Cory noticed that as well as being stubborn I was innately affectionate. I was a time-consuming charge, though not so labour-intensive as were the babies, of whom there was nearly always more than one. The social services paid the matron, Mrs Vernon, an extra allowance for every baby in the home – it was extra work.

None the less Cory's blue eyes already had a twinkle. She was serious-minded but also full of fun, wonderful with us children. In her tiny room at the back of Wormley Hill House, with its narrow bed and sparse furnishings, she continued to read childcare manuals. A bit lonely but ever resourceful, she bought a pet budgie, a blue one, who did cheer her up and seemed to enjoy looking out of the window. But after two months, Mrs Vernon decided the budgie was in the way, and it went to Hoddesdon, not many miles away to live with Cory's Mum and Dad.

The best snapshot I have of Cory shows her holding a smiling baby in the crook of one arm and holding on to me with the other. It is no wonder, with all she had to do, that her mouse-coloured hair looks stringy, probably slightly in need of a wash, with the fringe pushed back, away from her eyes. It was Cory's job to look after us. She did her job willingly and well.

I could be clingy and unreasonably demanding, so could many of the others – we were, most of us, disturbed children. But Cory managed. She put up with us all. Cory was the first person who ever showed me any love, but she had so many other children to

6

care for. She had to be there for all of them and not just for me.

I remember falling and hurting myself one afternoon – I couldn't have been more than four. But even as I lay sobbing on the ground in the small playing field at the back of the house, I knew Cory had a lot of us to look after, and I would have to wait my turn. When Cory finally came, she examined my scraped knee with exactly the right amount of concern and she made much of me. So it had been worth waiting for. It was on the makeshift playing fields of Wormley Hill that I learned the patience which I have had to call upon so frequently during my athletics career.

The children at the home were of all sorts, English, Nigerian, Cypriot. Some of them had been born in other parts of Britain but had been taken into care in Greater London. Some used to play joyfully. There were others who couldn't stop crying. We were a mixed bunch of sad little characters.

I don't remember many individuals. I was too young. But I'll never forget one blond-haired, chubby little boy called Michael. He wet the bed a lot and was always clutching on to a little red bus. Michael insisted it was his toy because he had been given it by his mother on one of her visits. He didn't want anyone else to have it, and would take it back from whomever was playing with it, hiding the bus under the carpet where it made a large bulge that was easy to trip over. But Michael could never understand how his hiding place was discovered.

Even our Christmas presents, nearly always second-hand things donated by the locals, were usually shared. But Cory's mother made me a yellow dress and sewed a name tag in it. It was a pale, almost a cream colour, with a pattern of little flowers. Cory sometimes had to rescue my dress from the communal laundry before it was put over the head of a girl in one of the other two play groups. With Cory's vigilance, I kept my dress, but inevitably Michael lost the battle of the red bus. His toy did become communal, and was soon broken by somebody.

Although I didn't know any other way of life, I resented the fact that I didn't have anything or anyone who was specially mine. It was an emotional hollow within, that longed to be filled. I was also aware of wanting very much to be an individual, and not

7

always to have to do things with eight other children, sometimes more.

Mornings, still in our pyjamas, we walked in a straggly single file down the corridor to the communal toilets, where I can vividly remember the babies in their potties shuffling across the floor, whilst we bigger children tried to muster more grown-up dignity as we crouched on child-sized toilets in one of the six cubicles which had no doors. We would attend the toilets in the morning and then following lunch and before going to bed. No one got up from their toilet until they had completed the allotted task. There was no privacy, of course, but we knew no sense of shame.

The bathroom was on the same floor, and when we had washed our faces and hands, we were allowed to walk back to our bedrooms on our own. There some of the children would wait on their beds to be dressed, but it was important to me that I dressed myself. This bid for independence was part of my desire to be an individual. I also realised, even then, that I needed to look after myself as no one really wanted or had the time to look after me.

There was, I am sure, another reason I showed my independence. After I dressed myself it was very nice to hear Cory tell me that I was a very good girl, which she would say even though, often as not, I put my jumper on back to front or inside out.

Once dressed, we would congregate at the top of the big staircase and make our way down to breakfast. This is where one morning when I was feeling down, I stopped being a good girl. I was feeling particularly bleak and unwanted and the 'baby of the moment', who had colic, had taken up a lot of Cory's time. To get some attention, at the top of the stairs I began to whimper and cry and loudly stamp my feet.

As the other children watched, eyes wide and disbelieving, I began to indulge in a tantrum – the kind of childish tantrum that makes most adults want to kill – screeching and kicking my heels. Cory merely wanted to quiet me. But I didn't respond to her overtures, and having her hands full with the baby and seven other little ones, she was at a loss as to know what to do. The din I was making was ear-piercing.

The matron poked her head out of the door of her lounge office

8

down below. She was a slender woman with an air of elegance. Her clothes had the classic, sophisticated look that was more Esher than our neighbouring metropolises of Hertford and Harlow. When Mrs Vernon went to the shops she slung a straw basket over her arm. No brown paper bags for her.

But her sophistication was beyond the comprehension of us children. Cory admired Mrs Vernon. To us, however, she was an austere presence, someone we heard talking to officials on the telephone at the little desk at the bottom of the stairs, but with whom we had little personal contact. To me Mrs Vernon seemed ancient, though she was probably on the verge of forty, give or take a few years. That day, the day of my first tantrum, I was making such a disturbance that Mrs Vernon took an interest. 'Stop it, Fatima,' she said firmly.

I continued to howl and stamp my feet, if anything even more insistently. The matron came out of her office. 'Stop it,' she said again, and then to Cory, 'Whatever are you doing to Fatima?'

Cory shrugged. 'I'm not doing anything to her, but I can't do anything with her either this morning, Mrs Vernon.'

So Mrs Vernon had to take me in hand, literally. Out she came, up all those stairs, just to see what was disturbing me. 'Don't be naughty, Fatima,' she said, and gave me a little cuddle. It was a perfunctory, professional cuddle, but a cuddle none the less. I reduced my decibel level, but I didn't stop crying entirely, and I continued to stamp my feet. Mrs Vernon gave me a quick little kiss on the forehead and took my hand. My tantrum had worked. It had got me what I wanted — some semblance of love and attention. This was it.

'I don't want any breakfast,' I said tearfully.

'But you do want a biscuit, don't you?' Mrs Vernon smiled reassuringly. 'Come along with me. I'll give you one.'

Walking down the stairs, taking my time because it was quite a big staircase, I felt quite pleased that all the other children were going on to breakfast and I was going to Mrs Vernon's special room.

There she gave me a biscuit and stood me by the fire where it was warm. She sat down in the big armchair, put me on her knee

9

and gave me another cuddle. I began to feel a lot better. That room was so different from the rest of the house, which was colder, more impersonal and institutional. I munched my biscuit as slowly as possible.

The next day, or perhaps it was a few days later, I had another tantrum at the top of the stairs. Mrs Vernon peered out of her office, saw what the disturbance was, and came out to the bottom of the stairs. 'Come on, Fatima, down you come, I've got something here in my office for you,' she said. It was a kiss, as perfunctory as before, and another cuddle and a lovely sugary biscuit. As I felt the warmth of the fire on my legs and prepared to bite into that biscuit, a big smile appeared on my face. I had triumphed.

So for a time this almost daily routine, which I liked rather more than many of the other routines at the home, continued. Cory and the rest of the children would be half way down the stairs. Cory would say 'Come on', and I wouldn't because I was waiting for matron to intervene.

That first tantrum was perceived as an act of rebellion. But it was something quite different, something more important than rebellion. It was my first act of self-assertion, my first clear-cut demand for what I craved almost as much as affection – recognition. Since I had no Mum and was not special to someone, I had to be someone special.

Although I was often denied the softness of cuddles when I wanted them, although I so often had to wait my turn, I had not grown used to it. And my illogical and instinctive tantrum was a declaration that I would not allow myself to become used to teaspoons of affection when I needed cupsful, that I would not accept emotional deprivation as my lot in life. Troublesome and annoying as tantrums might be, and naughty, they were the only way I had of saying that I knew who I was.

Even though I could sense I wasn't receiving the quality of affection the matron would have given a child of her own; even though I knew she was humouring me, I felt I had made my point. What I wanted was regular attention, attention on demand. She never offered it, but it was there, albeit mingily, when I demanded

10

it. It made my mornings something to get up for. It helped me get through the day. As I bit into the last of my biscuit, Mrs Vernon would say, 'Run along.'

Back I would saunter to the group, spooning up my cornflakes quickly and downing the glass of milk in big swallows so that I could play with the others for the half hour or so it took Cory to clear up the dishes and get the big ones off to school. Then, rain or shine, came the next item on our agenda, a two-mile trudge to the village. The distance was arduous for us little ones, but now that I think of it, it probably helped initiate me into the rigours of endurance training. Nowadays I run instead of walking, often with a tyre tied to a rope around my waist and dragging along behind. The purpose of our little walk, however, was to give us some fresh air, to tire us out and get us out of matron's way.

I would hold on to Cory's skirt as she pushed the pram with the baby in it, and all the other children trotted along behind. I don't mean that I was necessarily in front. We all used to trot along together, but as close to Cory as we could get.

There was a little wood we walked past and a park with swings. Then we would come to the village. I hated our arrival at the village because the villagers knew us, knew who we were. On the other hand I loved to go there because we would see other children with their parents, their mummies and daddies holding their hands. I would grip Cory's skirt tighter. She was all I had to hold on to.

During the two years I lived at Wormley Hill I cannot remember having one visit, not even from a social worker. But Cory tells me I was from time to time taken out for the day by prospective foster parents. Evidently, the chunky little girl with the dark eyes and hair didn't charm any of them. I was always put back on the shelf.

I did not know I had been abandoned, although I had heard things that probably I shouldn't have. I only knew I did not have a mummy like other children. Cory knew little of the details of my past, only that, as one of the staff put it, as a baby I had been 'dumped'. I don't know what makes someone what they are but I do know that even at that age I wanted something and there was a big gap in my life, something important missing. At four years old I was desperate.

11

It is my belief that I was more desperate, that I felt the loss more acutely than the other children did. But none of us was very happy. We all felt bereft in one way or another. We didn't talk about it. We were too young. Only every now and then, one of us would start to cry. Cory dreaded it, because it would catch like wildfire and soon all of us would be crying. She couldn't always jolly us out of it, but one of her more successful ploys was to sit us on the window ledge at the rear of the house, so we could look out into the garden and watch for cars along the small country road which ran alongside. Somehow it comforted us.

On other occasions I would go to the front of the house and look out of the big window, hoping and hoping that I would see someone walking up to the front door and that whoever it was was coming to take me away from my lonely existence. I used to look out of that window almost every day. If any ladies came to the door, I would jump up and down crying, 'This lady is going to be my new mummy!'

'Oh no, she's not going to be a new mummy,' Cory would say protectively. 'She's not come here to take anyone away. She's come here to see Mrs Vernon.' Cory knew I would find that a little more acceptable than when people came to the door to take another child away.

Then, I would say to Cory, 'Will you be my mummy?' and she would give me a kiss and a cuddle.

If not for Cory, I doubt that I would have turned out as well as I have. She was the most important person in my life. I suppose Mr and Mrs Vernon were important too, though I don't so much as remember Mrs Vernon's face and have no visual memory at all of Mr Vernon. But Cory showed me the first genuine kindness I ever knew. It was not enough, but I'll always be grateful to her for it.

Sometimes, of course, she couldn't protect me from seeing other children going away for the weekend or for a holiday with their mummies or daddies. And many parents would come to visit their children at the home for a few hours. I couldn't understand why I didn't have a mummy and daddy, and if I did, where were they?

Michael, the boy with the red bus, had a mother who loved

12

him but was unable to take care of him properly. She was ill, perhaps even mentally ill – it may even be that she abused him. I was too young to understand the nuances. But I remember clearly one of the days she visited him at the home. She cuddled him, and they were laughing and playing together. At the end of the visit she simply took him by the hand and walked out of the back door, and kept walking very quickly towards the road.

Somebody suddenly noticed. Then Cory and a few others began to run after them, calling out, 'Wait! Wait!'

But Michael and his mother kept going. They got to the fence and went out of the gate. Cory and the others were running towards them. They eventually caught them, and Michael like me had to stay at the home.

In the mornings, on the way back from the village, I often tried to climb into the pram. I said I was tired, but in truth I wanted to be babied. I remember a cold, dreary morning when three or four of us piled into the pram. Cory put the baby on top, and pushed us all the whole way back.

On our return, Mrs Vernon said her usual, 'Did you have a good walk in the fresh air and get plenty of exercise?'

'Yes, Mrs Vernon, very nice,' we answered more or less in unison, and had a little laugh to ourselves that we had tricked her.

The routine at Wormley Hill House was simple and fairly unvaried: the daily trips into the village, lunch, drawing pictures, trying to knit – I never learned how – outdoor play in the backyard, tea, bath and bedtime. When you have so many children to cater for routine is, perhaps unwittingly, used not just to pass the time but to fill the emotional spaces in the children's lives. And while on the one hand it can get you down – it used to affect me that way – on the other hand it was our security and a substitute for love, for everything.

After our morning constitutional I would be more than ready for lunch – normally some variety of baked beans with sausages and mash. During the blackberry season Cory augmented our diet with berries she picked either from just beyond the fence near the home or, if there weren't any ripe ones left there, from the hedgerows during our daily walks. She would put them in little

13

paper bags in the pram and the next morning there would be a sprinkling of blackberries to cheer up our cornflakes.

Thank goodness, though, that I was not a finicky eater. I was mostly eager to eat my meal, whatever it was. But if I wasn't I knew I had to eat up anyway. I learned that the hard way from Gloria, one of the other assistants. Unlike Cory, Gloria, who was a big, strong, young woman of about twenty, did not have a gentle nature. Gloria had charge of another group of children. She bossed them around, and when she could, she bossed us too.

One lunchtime I was not hungry and could not eat my meal.

'You are being naughty,' said Gloria threateningly. 'Eat up or I will see to it that you do.'

'I'm not being naughty. I'm not hungry.' I was crying. Perhaps I was being just a little naughty, but I had lost my appetite. It was one of those dull, thick wintery days when the sky is a terrible grey-white. The whole sky was like a huge, dirty loaf of bread, dreary. I was feeling dull inside too. I was too young to realise it consciously, but perhaps my stomach was telling me, instinctively, that the emptiness I felt that day couldn't be filled by food.

'Eat up,' Gloria said. 'Or I'll make you.'

'I'm not hungry,' I repeated in a whine, expecting another entreaty.

But coaxing wasn't in Gloria's nature. Force was. Suddenly she put her body weight against me and held my arms around the back of me. As I struggled, squirming to get away, she shoved the spoon at my moving head.

I tried harder to fight her off. So my nose was held and food was thrust down my throat. I coughed and spluttered and spat it out, but she kept on at me. It was a rough and untidy affair in the dining room in front of everybody. The other children kept on eating. She didn't get much food down me, but she made her point. I got a few spanks too.

I don't suppose it was anything to do with the food. What does a young child do when she feels completely and utterly empty yet at the same time brimming over with the knowledge that she has to do the same thing everyday and it is never the one thing she wants to do, which is be with her mummy?

14

I didn't learn my lesson immediately. Gloria took it upon herself to force feed me again. But I soon learned.

On such occasions I would cheer myself up by running down to the edge of the garden where the wonderful birds were. The neighbours had a splendid aviary which we were sometimes allowed to visit. That was an enjoyment, and one of the few bright spots in my life. There were peacocks. The colours were gorgeous and bold. I would want to sneak in – we weren't always allowed to. I felt more at home visiting the birds than walking into the village, and I was fascinated that there could be beautiful, colourful things like that in life.

I liked our drawing sessions too, although it certainly wasn't the colour that engrossed me. With a stub of crayon clenched in my hand, I would sit hunched thoughtfully over the long wooden table, staring at a large blank sheet of paper, deciding what to draw. The drawing paper we used was the reverse side of wallpaper. Rolls of it had been contributed to the home and Cory had cut it up into smaller sizes.

Before I started my picture, I would examine the pale blue of the playroom walls on which the best pictures of the day before were still hanging. While trying to decide what to draw, something that would merit display, I would gaze out of the window at the pink and purple of the shrubs or at grey sky. Our playroom was a room with a view, but only rarely would I attempt to draw any part of this rural vista. Instead, I would draw the other children – and sometimes Cory – the park and the swings with one of us going high, and the baby in the pram. Cory used sticky tape to put the best pictures on the wall. It wasn't so much the drawing that I enjoyed, it was getting my picture chosen to go on the wall. That was nice. I would think proudly, 'that's mine'. It was important to me to be acknowledged as doing something good.

I was usually a good girl during drawing, but at other times I suppose you could say that I was a handful. There were many tantrums at the top of the stairs – or elsewhere. I seem to remember that sometimes I was so naughty that I was sent to the barn. I didn't like the barn at the best of times. Even when we played

15

there on rainy afternoons, I would much rather have been outside. The worst of times was when I was banished there.

I remember one occasion in particular when I was in there for some severe breach of discipline – at that home there was a good deal of discipline to breach – and it must have been winter, because darkness fell early. The barn suddenly seemed to me perilously far from the house. Wormley Hill was at a leafy crossroads two miles from the village, in the country really, and at night there was no light anywhere. The barn seemed huge, and it was pitch dark. I was four going on five.

The direst part of the punishment was that the other children were together in the safety of the big house. I was sure that the bogy man would get me, or ghosts would, or some creepy-crawly. The barn was also too far away for me to hear what was going on in the house, but I imagined I could hear them playing, Cory holding Michael or the baby on her knee. They would be having a good time, feeling secure, and with me out in the wilderness hearing all these windy, whirly sounds and the trees whispering dangerously.

At last I was called in for the evening meal. Bathtime, which was wonderful, followed. The baths were huge and old-fashioned, made of white porcelain, with feet. They were so deep it was hard to get in and out, and so big we bathed two at a time, two girls or two boys.

We children played games – the splashing water went every-where – and Cory entered into the fun, as she always did. But she also made sure we washed our necks and behind our ears very thoroughly.

I adored water. I also remember very clearly the rare warm, fine days of summer when most of the young ones were put into buckets of water outdoors and the older children would run around the back garden with the hose pipe spraying each other.

Bathtime was only slightly more sedate. When we finished our turn in the bath, I and the child with whom I had shared the tub dried ourselves while the next two were bathing. And then off we went to bed, promptly at seven o'clock.

My bed was in the rear of the room, away from the door. I felt

16

much more secure tucked away in a corner like that than in the middle of the room.

That night, after being in the barn, I wet the bed. I woke up wet and cold. I hated to wet the bed. I knew the rules: in the morning I would have to strip the bed and put the sheets in a pile. I hoped I wouldn't do it again the next night, because if I became a regular everyone would know.

The baby's cot was near the corner where my bed was. Often the baby would cry in the night. Cory slept in the staff quarters upstairs, so I used to get out of bed and climb into the cot to see if the baby was all right. If he had dropped his dummy, I retrieved it. I was now nearly five, one of the big ones with responsibilities.

But at bedtime I would often have a cry. Other children would be crying too. Of course there were times when we were too sleepy to cry or when we would play games secretly, and have something approaching a good time.

The only other house I remember visiting during the entire time that I lived at Wormley Hill was Cory's parents' house, where from time to time Cory would take me for the day, or even for the weekend. Cory never took any of the other children. I loved to go.

After she helped me on with my coat, I would pull the striped mittens, which she had knitted for me from oddments of wool, out of the sleeves where they hung by a string, and put them on. Then we went out of the back door, and through the fence.

There was a little game of pretend I used to play as Cory and I walked to Wormley village together, just the two of us, and caught the bus to her town of Hoddesdon two villages away. I imagined that I was with my mummy and we were going back to our house.

It wasn't a long bus ride to Cory's village. When we got there, we would pop into the shops to pick up a few things for our meal. There were many young children out with their mummies, and, once, as I waited for Cory to make our purchases, I remember seeing a little girl a bit bigger than me, but not much, who had Cory's colour hair and whose mummy was just ahead of Cory in the queue. The girl made a face at me and I scowled at her, but I could tell she thought I was with my mummy just like she was.

On this occasion whatever we were buying took longer to get than we expected. We had to hurry along the busy high street to visit Cory's mother at work at Hayward's, the ironmonger's shop. Cory's mother, Elsie Muddle, was a thicker-set, ever-so-slightly taller version of Cory. I liked her instantly. And Mrs Muddle, an East Ender by birth, who stood not much above five foot nothing, transmitted huge signals of warmth across the hardware counter. But we couldn't stay long. There were customers waiting, and besides Cory and I had to hurry home to prepare the tea for the rest of the family when they got home.

'Come along,' said Cory, as I looked into shop windows, enthralled by the sights of Hoddesdon, a town, not just a village like Wormley. 'There's no time today for dawdling. Come along, Fats.' Fats was short for Fatima. I wasn't particularly fat, and didn't even realise the implications of my nickname. I don't think Cory did either. I hurried along after her, willing to please.

But as we passed the sweetshop with its tall glass jars of loose sweets gleaming in the window – sugary chocolate marbles, jellies (my favourite) and, somewhere inside, Maltesers – I stopped dead in my sandals.

'I want sweets,' I bleated.

'You don't want sweets just before your tea,' replied Cory.

'Sweets, I want sweets.' I wouldn't give up.

'We have some at home.' Cory pulled me along. 'Fatima, you can have them after tea.'

'I *want* sweeeets,' I howled. I went into one of my obnoxious stamping of feet routines. 'Sweeeets.'

Cory was embarrassed and annoyed. 'Stop it now, Fatima,' she said.

I continued to stamp my feet and shout. After all, this was the behaviour that usually elicited biscuits. Why not sweets? But instead, to my amazement, Cory smacked my legs. To this day I remember the sting which was not great and my surprise which was gargantuan. I was so startled by the fact that she had smacked me that I immediately stopped being a nuisance. Cory had never

18

hit me before. Nor do I remember her ever having to smack me again.

After tea, which was a hot meal and plenty of it, eaten round a table with her parents and two younger sisters, Ann and Leona, Cory, true to her promise, gave me a little bag of jellies. I clutched them in my fingers. I still like sweets. I remember sucking my sweets as I leaned against the imitation green brick wall in the lounge, then moving further away from the oil fire, surveying this house where Cory had lived since she was four years old. Sometime later, Cory painted her fingernails and mine shocking pink.

I wish I could remember more about Leo Muddle, Cory's dad, who had twinkly blue eyes like Cory's and hair almost as dark as mine. By trade he was a wire welder, who put the delicate finishing touches on umbrella and lampshade frames, but he was a hefty fellow who towered over all of us. I was playing in the lounge on the brightly patterned carpet when he came home, and I remember him picking me up, seemingly effortlessly and sitting me on his lap. I liked it. He was strong. He smelled different from Cory and her mother, from all the grown-ups I knew. They were all women. This was the first time I had ever received any affection from a man. It felt good.

Cory's father believed strongly that something should be done to improve conditions at the children's home. A men's club he belonged to, called the Buffs, would raise money for the home, or take us on outings.

Cory could be very effective too. At one stage the prams which were used to convey the younger children on their morning safari became so dilapidated that she placed a notice in a shop in Hoddesdon, requesting people who no longer needed such items to donate them. Overwhelmed with replies, we received a number of what to us were luxury vehicles. But the best pram, much to Cory's annoyance, was given by Mrs Vernon to one of the other play groups.

Cory was getting attached to me, as I was to her. I kept saying I wanted her to be my mummy. I never resented other children but I never really wanted her to give the other children the love she gave to me, because then I would feel just like one of those children. I wanted to be special. It was selfish to want Cory to myself, holding my hand, putting me on her lap, taking just me out. That couldn't be.

Cory left Wormley after nine or ten months there, six months before I did. It was Cory's parents who persuaded her to leave the home as they felt that she was not having the opportunity to lead a teenager's life. I often think that her parents may have sensed that during the time she was at Wormley Hill House she was becoming too attached to a little girl called Fatima who constantly pleaded with her to become her mummy.

A few months after Cory had left the home to work elsewhere her father's club, the Buffs, arranged a special trip to the zoo for the children at the home. Cory came along to help. It is easy to forget faces at that age, and someone else was doing Cory's job of looking after us, but almost as soon as she walked in the door, I ran up to her and grabbed her skirt, saying, 'You are my new mummy. I want you to be my mummy.' She was very good to me, but she made it clear that it wasn't to be.

Cory went on to become a nanny. Later she and her husband emigrated to New Zealand and her parents followed. Now Cory lives in Hertfordshire again, a javelin's throw from Wormley, and not only has two children of her own, Brett and Glenn, but works mornings in her husband's office and finds time to model in local fashion shows – she still has that rangy, *haut couture* shape. Not only that, Cory teaches keep-fit in the evenings. Could it be that I inherited my physical stamina from her? Well, not literally, of course, but she did set me a good example. Part of her legacy to me too was the belief that someone could love me, and that surely was a prelude to me myself learning how to love.

It was Cory who rediscovered *me* eighteen years after she left Wormley. Watching the Helsinki World Championships on television in the summer of 1983, she saw me win a silver medal and weep in my mother's arms, and something clicked. When, to her amazement, the name Fatima Whitbread flashed on the screen, she said to her husband, 'Could that be my Fatima?'

They both thought it unlikely, as Cory's Fatima didn't have a

20

mother. But later a neighbour told Cory she had read that Fatima Whitbread grew up in a children's home.

'But was she dumped?' Cory asked.

The neighbour found the article which confirmed I had been abandoned. Cory wrote to me, asking if I was 'the naughty little girl' she used to care for. When I replied excitedly that I was, she sent me some wonderful snapshots from those bad old days.

We met in the flesh the following year, when in the run-up to the Los Angeles Olympics there was a television documentary about my life. Much of the programme was of me in a chauffeured limousine *en route* to Buckingham Palace where I was to collect the Sybil Abrahams trophy for achievement at sport. It was the first of many times I was to win that award, one that I value highly, and it was my first visit to the palace, but I can assure you, I was just as thrilled at seeing my Cory, who is now Mrs Paul Boswell.

Cory looked very chic. Her hair was nicely done-up and, I think, a bit blonder. Seeing her was a very emotional experience. She said I was her favourite, which I knew. I grinned when I heard her say, 'Fatima was a tough little girl, very strong and very strong-willed.' Cory and I are still in touch.

One evening just before bedtime at Wormley I was told by Mrs Vernon that I was to be ready at nine o'clock the next morning as my social worker was coming to take me to join my brother and sister in a new home. I was five years old.

I had not been aware until then that I had a brother or a sister. Years later I found out that the brother in question, Adem, who was three years older than me, was even a member of my group at Wormley for about two weeks. Cory remembers him as a troubled little boy with a chip on his shoulder. Because of 'a lesson' someone had taught him, perhaps painfully, he wouldn't call her by name, but insisted on calling her Nurse. At the time, since he wasn't staying on, the social services had felt it unwise to inform us of each other's identities.

Suddenly there seemed to have been a change in policy.

That night I could hardly sleep. Whenever I dozed I would wake up abruptly, thinking it's my last night here, I'm leaving. I

21

knew I didn't want to go. It was not because there was any particular child here whom I would miss. We were and we weren't friends. Most of us were so troubled that we lived in our own little worlds. Besides, you never knew which of them would be gone the next day. Many of the children were transients. Some would go home to their parents occasionally or they might be fostered. They passed through. After two years there, at the age of five, I was one of the veterans. What I sensed that I was going to miss far more than the people was the feeling of familiarity and the security of Wormley Hill House.

Although it was a creaky old house, very impersonal and I wasn't all that happy there, it was still the only home I could remember living in, and everyone I knew well in the world lived there. During the night, I dreamed that a scarey figure in a dark cloak was walking up and down the corridor, clanging a bell and looking for me. I wet my bed.

The next morning I stripped the sheets and blankets and placed them dutifully at the foot of the bed. I hoped that I wouldn't wet the strange new bed I would be sleeping in that night. It would make a bad first impression.

3

Moved On

As I marched with the other children in single file to the bathroom, I thought, 'this is the last time.' I didn't mind that. On the way down the stairs to breakfast, I didn't bother to make the usual fuss – stamping my feet on the floor and screeching for attention from Mrs Vernon was now a waste of time. I was leaving.

No one seemed to notice me stirring my cornflakes round and round in the chipped bowl instead of eating them. No one seemed to care that my stomach was in a painful knot of confusion. As quickly as possible I left the table and was ready, as I had been told to be, by nine o'clock, standing in the reception corner of the front hall. No one had arrived to see me. I sat down on the bottom step of the staircase and craning my head up to see the ceiling on the third floor landing, I waited.

I had on the yellow dress Cory's mother had made me. The other personal items that I had acquired – an almost matching cardigan which came from the communal wardrobe, my tooth-brush, a change of underwear and another dress from the communal pile – were in the brown paper bag beside me.

I waited and waited. Of necessity I was a patient five-year-old. I could hear all the other children playing in an adjoining room. Soon they would be departing for the morning promenade to the village. I wished I was going with them. Today there was no need for coats or to search for mittens in your sleeves. My cardie seemed an unnecessary appendage, but I had been told to take it.

It was the hot, dry summer of 1966. A summer for the record books. Not just fair, not just fine, but Italy in the streets. Sitting in the foyer was almost sinful on a day like that.

23

An hour that seemed like 20,000 decades passed. I felt lonely. No one came to see if I was all right. If I was leaving, I wanted to leave, and if I was staying, I wanted to be playing with the others.

The clock struck ten. Well after that the doorbell rang. Mrs Vernon brushed past me to open the front door, and I heard the social worker say she had come to see me and was sorry to be late.

Mrs Vernon ushered in two women – a bland, pleasant woman whom I vaguely remembered as the social worker who had originally brought me to Wormley and with her a fat woman with too much hair and perfume and a gold front tooth. I could smell the scent she was wearing even before she entered the house. None of the women at the home wore scent. I had never seen the fat woman before. I didn't like the look of her.

'Fatima,' the social worker said cheerily, 'this is your mother. She is coming with us to help you meet your brother and sister.'

'She is not my mummy.' I announced with certainty. 'I don't have a mummy or daddy.'

The fat woman didn't pick me up. She didn't hug me. She didn't show any affection. She was not what I had been waiting for all these years.

As we walked to the car I stuck close to the social worker, taking her hand. Mrs Vernon said goodbye matter-of-factly, as if we were going for a trip to the park. I said goodbye back. I wasn't up to a tantrum. I may have looked as blank as I felt. Squeezing my hand, the social worker said, 'It will be an easy journey.' She put me in the front seat beside her. She put the fat woman in the back.

The journey was long and painful. The social worker kept telling me that I would enjoy myself in the countryside in Essex and to look out the window at the trees and animals as we drove along. There was no real conversation in the car. At one point the woman who they said was my mother spoke, in broken English with a strong foreign accent. All these years I had wanted a mummy, but the one I wanted wasn't her. I didn't recognise her. I felt no relation to her. Nor did she seem to feel anything for me. I was crying a little.

As the car sped along, I continued to look out of the window, where the cows and horses and the fields kept vanishing. After a time, the social worker said cheerfully, 'We're almost there.' Out of the window there were flat streets crammed with small houses, each very like the other. It was a new town, like Harlow which was quite near, with a spill-over of East Enders.

'It's just here somewhere,' the social worker said, driving slowly. 'Your brother and sister will be waiting for you, Fatima.'

The woman in the back said, 'I want to see them.'

The social worker turned into a street of large semis and parked the car. Pulling me past the modest front garden towards the front door, she said, in a voice that I found unconvincing, 'You're really going to enjoy being here.'

As she rang the doorbell, I stood hiding behind her, paper bag in hand, on the side furthest from the woman they said was my mother. The door was opened by the matron, an elderly lady who looked strict, and we were ushered in.

The social worker and the other woman were led into the garden 'where Adem and Aliya are, your brother and sister.'

I was left alone in the hallway, wondering if I really had a brother and sister and what they might be like. I feared that further shocks might await me – a very numbed and frightened five-year-old girl – at this house, where I was to spend the next eight years of my life. During a period of less than twenty-four hours I had been told that I was moving away from the only people and the only place I knew to a new home, and that I had a brother and a sister. Then, suddenly, I was confronted with a mother who couldn't possibly be mine. She didn't look like a mother, and certainly not mine. My whole upbringing had been that of a British girl. The songs and nursery rhymes we were taught by the assistants were traditional. The staples of our diet were sausage and mash or baked beans. The biscuit we were most frequently given as a treat was a digestive. I knew about the flag and the Queen. And the people I saw in the village and who reared me tended to have mouse-coloured hair like Cory's and snub noses. They certainly didn't wear blobs of garish lipstick or have gold teeth.

It had never occurred to me that my background was anything but British. I felt British through and through. So this foreign woman couldn't possibly be my mother. In retrospect, I think that I would have reacted very negatively to my mother whoever she was. I must have been deeply angry at having been left in a children's home. What I had been asking for was a *new* mummy, not one who hadn't wanted me in the first place.

But I doubt that I understood any of this as I stood alone in the hallway of what was going to be my new home. The hallway was tiny compared to the one in the house I came from. This whole house was small. Compared to Wormley, it was austere, mingy. I didn't like the look of the place. Not only that. The house appeared to be empty of children.

Returning from the garden, the stern, unsmiling matron began to settle me in, taking me first to the bedroom where I would be sleeping from now on. There were five metal beds in the room, and a small locker next to each bed. This was the girls' room. The boys' room, which was almost identical, had one bed less and was across the hall. I was given the bed under the window, which I didn't like. It was too easy for the wild beasts and ghosts and other scary things in the night to get to you. They could climb in the window and you would be right there, defenceless.

The bathroom, which was further along the hallway, was much smaller than the one at Wormley Hill. Each child's toothbrush was in a plastic beaker, which had the child's name taped to it. There was a piece of plaster with my name on it and the matron attached it to a spare beaker. There were nine of them there, lined up in a row. On the way down the stairs, which weren't particularly steep or long or special, the matron gave me a little lecture about the queue for the bathroom in the mornings. It was in strict order of age. 'You must not rush to the front of the queue.' Her pinched voice confirmed my suspicion that she would be a stickler for rules, 'and always wait your turn.'

Another thing I was not to do was to enter the lounge without her permission, none of the children could; and under no circumstances could anyone except herself switch on the television. This latter bit of information was actually promising. The only TV

26

at Wormley had been in the Vernons' flat. We children hadn't had access to it at all.

Through the open French windows of the dining room I could see the social worker sitting in the sun. There were six or eight children out there, playing in the garden. And the fat woman they said was my mother was talking to two of them, a skinny, dark-haired little girl who wore spectacles and a boy who was stocky but had the same dark hair. The woman was cuddling the girl.

The matron led me over to meet my supposed sister and brother. As we approached, the girl took off her spectacles and I could hear the three of them talking in a language I did not understand.

'This is Aliya,' the matron said, indicating the girl who was blinking a little and holding her spectacles by their pink plastic frames. 'And this is Adem.' The boy glowered at me fiercely, as if to say I don't care who you are. I gave him the same unfriendly look. He was bigger and older than his sister or even than me. 'And this is your sister Fatima. Say "Hello".'

We said 'Hello'. I felt no affinity towards them, and no doubt they felt likewise.

My supposed mother told us in broken English that she loved us all and that as soon as she had enough money she would take us home to join our other brother and sister. Now it seemed I also had another brother and sister who lived in North London.

In later years I was told that Adem, who was three years older than I, and Aliya, who was eighteen months younger, were fathered by one man, that another man was responsible for my arrival on earth and that a third man fathered the two younger children, Emmie and Metin.

The social worker, whom I had found to be quite a nice person, now said that they had to be going, and that she was certain that I would be happy here. I wasn't. I had always thought that when I left Wormley it would be to go and live with my new mummy and daddy in their house. It was a terrible blow to find myself at another children's home. I felt bewildered and frightened. I had to learn new house rules and make new friends. I had to start all over again.

The woman they said was my mother gave Adem and Aliya

each a kiss and said, 'Mummy love you.' Then she gave me a smile – the gold tooth showed – and walked off.

I wanted to hold the social worker's hand and go back with her. As for the supposed mother, well, she could go to hell. I went up to my room and had a cry.

When I look back upon this period, I am convinced the social services could have handled the situation differently.

The next morning I found that toothpaste had been applied in a neat, thin line to each toothbrush to ensure that we all used just enough and that none was wasted. I had not wet the bed the first night.

Routine was as important here as at Wormley. There were less than half as many children, but there was less than a quarter of the space. We were, in comparison with Wormley, packed together like pilchards in a tin. Making friction even greater was the fact that our age range was considerably larger, from a baby in a cot to, on occasion, teenagers of fifteen or sixteen. The room known as the girls' bedroom was the bigger of the two children's bedrooms, but, as I found out later, whenever there were more boys than girls living in the house we switched rooms.

The elderly spinster who was in charge was very strict and seemed to like us children best when we were out of sight and earshot. She was nearing retirement age. It may be that we were getting to be too much for her. She could not tolerate us playing in the house: we were too noisy. This was fine on dry days when we played in the garden, where there was a swing. I loved swinging.

There were fruit trees too, tantalizingly near our garden, which we were strictly forbidden to climb. But as soon as the first apples were ripe for picking, I shinnied up the tree and helped myself. I liked climbing trees and the trophy was delicious. I wasn't caught that time, but I was the next.

The punishment for such an offence was to sit for bum-aching hours on the back porch. The matron was a keen disciplinarian. I sat and sat, bored and indignant, until long after dark, when as well as all that I was frightened too. When she finally decided to go to bed, matron opened the door and let me come in. I hated the punishment. None the less, that summer I was always being caught up the tree helping myself to the apples.

When the weather was cold or wet, we were sent to play in the garage, which was attached to the house. Unheated, with floor and walls of concrete and large wooden doors, the garage made a cramped, chilly and not very comfortable playroom. As the heat wave continued throughout the summer, I was spared the garage until autumn. But that was too soon for me.

The garage, which was big enough for two cars, had not been converted in any way. We put together our jigsaw puzzles, which never had all the pieces, on the dirty floor, where some hand-me-down toys and leggo were also strewn.

The younger children would often cry because of the cold and I took it upon myself to go as a deputation of one to the matron to ask if we might come indoors. I suppose, I must have made it a demand rather than a request. Diplomacy was not my strong point.

'Stay there until you're called,' she said. 'And I want peace and quiet. No noise.'

It was clear that I was never going to be her favourite charge.

When we were finally allowed into the house we all had to wash our hands and faces, and a tea of jam sandwiches was presented and wolfed down. I enjoyed it at first, but after a while I became quite tired of jam sandwiches.

Bedtime was never later than six p.m., and no talking was allowed once we were in bed. Children being children there were pillow fights and obviously a lot of chatting and giggling. I settled in very quickly there, and was, I suppose, rambunctious.

Within a matter of weeks, the matron, being no fool, began to shout from the bottom of the stairs, 'Fatima, you are the ringleader. Come down here!' Then I would be banished to the porch, in my pyjamas, until she decided to go to bed. As I was still petrified of the dark, this was torture. If I was lucky, I might be exiled only to the stairs inside the house where the dangers were lesser. But these stairs were covered in a plastic material which had ridges in it and left a set of impressions on my backside.

The punishment was alternately scary and excruciatingly boring. And usually I was ravenous. Each evening before bed we were allowed two biscuits, one plain and one chocolate digestive. The matron kept count of the biscuits. We could also have a glass of watered-down, warm milk. Even though it was in addition to tea, this wasn't enough for me. I was always hungry in that house.

Matron kept all the biscuits in one big tin, which it was often my chore to refill. One day I noticed that she kept count only of the chocolate ones. When it was my turn again to do the refilling, I sneaked three of the chocolate ones to the bottom, where I placed them with the digestive side up. When she made her count, matron didn't notice the switch.

The next time that I was exiled to the porch, I felt exhilarated even though it was cold and dark and I didn't like it out there. I had a plan. I waited a good long while, fifteen minutes, perhaps half an hour, until I saw the gleam of the television on in the lounge. Matron was watching her programmes.

Stealthily I opened the back door and crept into the kitchen. To the left of the door was the cupboard where the biscuit tin was kept. I undid the lid, rescued the chocolate biscuits from the bottom and returned to the back doorstep where I sat happily munching away.

This became a habit. I was always being naughty. I wanted to do what I wanted to do. But I wasn't nasty.

Adem was. He and Aliya stuck close to each other and spoke to each other in that funny language. Occasionally Adem would try and push me around. He tried to lock me into the tiny cloakroom under the stairs where there was no light. Some of the children thought it was funny to push each other in and shut the door from outside but for me it was terrifying because of my fear of the dark. I fought him off.

'You're not our sister, our mother doesn't love you,' he would say. He was trying to bully me, but I wouldn't be pushed around. I would stand up to him. But what he said about her not loving me was quite obvious to me on the occasions when she turned up to take them home for the weekend. Even to Aliya, who was her favourite, the woman's arrival was a mixed blessing, because she would make the girl remove her spectacles and Aliya couldn't see a thing without them. The woman thought they made her look ugly.

I continued to have nightmares, triggered no doubt by some noise in the corridor in the night, but also a reflection of my inner fear. There was one nightmare that recurred over and over and which I still very occasionally have to this day. It was the frightening spectre of an eerie person in a cloak who was ringing a bell. The bell was attached to a long chain, which he or she – probably he but it wasn't certain – rang and rang. The chain was like the one that was used to flush our toilets. It may be that the dream was keeping me from wetting the bed. I don't know. Certainly it must have had further significance as I grew older.

I would wake up terrified, thinking strange creatures, ghosts, all the usual bogies of childhood, were coming to get me. I remember hiding under the bedclothes waiting for morning, often imagining that there were dangerous Red Indians hiding in the hallway, preparing to send their powerful arrows soaring through the corridor at me. I had not yet heard of a javelin.

Sometimes I did wet the bed when I had nightmares or if I felt very depressed or lonely. Bedwetters were made to feel dirty and disgusting. It was even worse here than at Wormley. You had to strip the bedclothes, of course, and the following night you were made to sit on the end of your bed until the matron was ready to retire and could send you for a final visit to the toilet. You weren't supposed to go to sleep before this, in case you had an accident. If you were a regular, you had to do that every night.

Some of the really young children couldn't stay awake in these circumstances. So what I used to do was stay awake for them, because the matron used to be very bad tempered with them and smack their legs if they fell asleep before she said they could. I would talk to the 'culprit', whispering, because if I was heard I would be summoned downstairs. When the child fell asleep, I would try to stay half awake, so that when I heard matron turn the television and the light off, I could wake the little girl up and tell her to sit up because 'Auntie', as we used to call the matron, was coming up. Even so, the poor little thing would be half asleep

31

when matron entered. She would then be shaken awake and made to go to the toilet.

The woman who said she was my mother visited me before Christmas and brought me a bag of Liquorice Allsorts, which matron immediately took out of my hand, saying they had to be kept for the proper time. Leaving the Liquorice Allsorts with matron, who said she would return them to me at Christmas, the woman took Aliya and Adem home with her for the holiday. I never saw those sweets again.

It was my first Christmas at the home. As was the policy, we each received one present. I can't remember what I got, but I can remember a Christmas tree with lights. Among the decorations hanging on the tree, were chocolates wrapped in foil, and whenever no one was looking, I would reach up on tiptoe, but I could not quite reach high enough to pull any off. Anyway, I didn't think it would go down very well.

That same Christmas there was a bowl of fruit on the window ledge. Hungry though I was, I knew better than to eat the fruit. Matron would have been angry. But I used to touch the fruit, tempted. One evening my finger went through the skin of an orange. It needed eating. I sucked out as much juice as I possibly could, and replaced the orange in the dish, with its puncture wound facing the window. When this crime was discovered and no one owned up immediately, we were all sent to bed.

I decided to confess.

'You're a very naughty, naughty girl,' said matron. She was disgusted with me. 'Go and sit on the porch. The children will stay where they are for the evening and you can see what a naughty girl you have been.' So the other children remained confined to their beds and she had an excuse to have some extra peace and quiet.

After the holiday, Aliya returned, but Adem was sent to another home as he was difficult to control.

I started at the nearby primary school during my first year at the home and I joined the local Brownie pack. School was a mixed blessing. My teacher at the infants' school would sometimes sit me on her lap when she was reading a story to the class. I liked that. But seeing other children's mummies and daddies giving them a morning kiss and cuddle before they went into school often upset me. It made me feel that I was different. On special occasions like open days and plays, when parents came to school, I felt very much an outsider.

Although there must have been many children whose parents did not deign to come to the school, or who could not come because they were working or ill, it never occurred to me that there were other children in much the same warped and leaky boat as I was. Even though I felt that the mother whom they had brought me when I was leaving Wormley was a nightmare instead of a dream come true, I don't think I ever realised that girls and boys who lived at home with their parents might be maltreated and forlorn.

Although I still wanted a mummy, I no longer expected ever to have one. And certainly after waiting for so long, I wasn't going to accept the imposter. I had learned to live without a mummy.

The Brownie pack had no drawbacks at all. Because Brown Owl, whose daughter was in our pack, worked in a children's home herself – it was just around the corner from where I lived – she understood my problems of adjustment and quietly made allowances. In the area there was a cluster of children's homes full of children from London councils. If only I had been sent to Brown Owl's.

Now that I think of it, Brown Owl was about as hefty as the woman they said was my mother, but as a child I never even noticed. Obviously, it wasn't really my so-called mother's figure that I found grotesque.

Going to school and the weekly Brownie meeting were the only occasions when I was allowed outside the home, except very rarely when we went as a group to the park.

One cool, damp Saturday morning, as I lay sprawled on the filthy, concrete floor of the garage, piecing together a jigsaw puzzle with a few of the others, I got increasingly restless. Several pieces of the puzzle were missing, which added to my sense of wishing I were somewhere else.

Some of the children were arguing over who should ride the scooter in that cramped space. A few others were trying to draw pictures with their gnawed bits of crayon. It was fairly cold in there, and very boring. I threw a piece of the puzzle across the garage. It didn't go far, but further than I had expected it to. I threw another piece. Then another. A few of the others joined in. We threw the whole puzzle across the garage. What a mess. Some of the children, who were drawing, folded their paper into aeroplanes, and threw them too. I picked up one of the planes and threw it as hard as I could across the garage. It didn't go far. 'It's a bird, it's a plane, it's Superman!' I shouted.

Now we were all shouting, throwing planes and bits of puzzle and dolls. Hoops. Crayons. Whatever was at hand. It was the most fun I had had yet in the garage. Better than a pillow fight. And there was no come-uppance either. We got away scot-free.

The only better memory I have of the garage was the time I sneaked out. I was bored with chucking pieces of puzzle, I guess. Before I quite realised what I was doing, and without a word to anyone, I strolled casually over to the door, and slipped out. Keeping well down so that the matron couldn't see me, I climbed over the neighbours' wall, and hid in the shadow of the four trees till I was out of the matron's line of vision. Then I walked jauntily up the road into the park, which was quite near. It was magic. You could run and run and run without coming up against a garden wall.

I was excited to be out on my own for once, and eager to see what was going on. A group of boys, who weren't from the home and who were a little older than me, were playing on a tyre swing. The tyre was tied by a rope to the limb of one of the biggest trees in the park, and they were swinging from side to side and backwards and forwards like Tarzan. When someone gave you a good hard push, you swung towards another big tree, which you could touch with your feet.

'I want a go,' I said.

The boys told me I was too small. When I persisted, they

ignored me. They knew I was one of the children from the home. One of them was big and noisy but most of them were not that much bigger than me.

'I want to have a go,' I repeated.

No notice was taken.

'Want a go, want a go, want a go!' I chanted over and over, and ran very close to where the swing was.

'Get out of the way,' the older boy said. 'You're too little. You'll get hurt.'

I wouldn't give up. I did a variation on my tantrum routine, not exactly stamping my feet, but staying underfoot. If I couldn't swing, they couldn't.

'Right,' the older one said at last. 'Have a go then. Straight away.'

I hadn't actually expected him to give in. I was a little scared.

'Straight away,' he said. 'I dare you.'

I sat down in the tyre, my legs barely touching the ground. 'Hold tight,' the boy said, and pushed me. I got a good lift and was just beginning to enjoy myself when the other tree loomed. I forgot to put out my feet – maybe I *was* too young – and crashed, right shoulder first, smack into the middle of the tree. I fell to the ground.

My pride was bruised as were my arm and shoulder, but nothing was dislocated or broken. I didn't cry much – the boys were watching. I was trying to be brave. But those boys made it all too easy. As soon as they realised nothing dire was wrong with me, they went on playing, and I ran along home.

My arm and shoulder ached for days, but I didn't dare tell anyone. At bathtimes I hid the few scratches and the big bruise. I knew better than to try to get any sympathy. I had to keep it a secret. If I said anything to anyone, the matron would hear of it, and I would be punished for leaving the garage. At the time I didn't see the irony of the situation, and felt hard done by. It was not my very first sports injury. I had fallen before when running in the back garden. But this one was my first lingering injury. Over the years, there would be all too many more.

My immediate concern, however, was the changing of the guard at the home. Matron was retiring. Taking her place would be Mrs Smith, a young married woman, who was due to arrive with her husband.

4

No Joke

The new matron introduced cod-liver oil. Everyone had to swallow a teaspoon full each morning before leaving for school. Marmite on our breakfast toast was another unpopular innovation. But there were no complaints at all about the new swing, which was put up in the garden alongside the one we already had. I wasn't the only one who loved to play on the swings. The new climbing frame was a hit too, and we got bicycles. Some old bicycles were given to the home and some were bought secondhand. There were even some more second-hand scooters for the younger children.

We were not banished to the garage anymore to play either. It was not at all difficult to oblige Mrs Smith when she said we must call her Auntie Brenda. She also asked us to call her husband Uncle Alan. Although he had a job during the day, we were to regard both of them as our houseparents.

For the first time in ages, I was happy. I should have known it couldn't last.

Auntie Brenda, a fairly hefty woman who wore her hair pulled back in a ponytail, was always flashing her oddly crooked smile at us those first few days. There was something the matter with the lower part of her face which was slightly twisted, as though she had suffered a stroke. She must have been about thirty, as was Uncle Alan, who was skinnier. A real stringbean who wore thick, horn-rimmed glasses, he combed his black hair over his forehead Buddy Holly-style.

At about the time the Smiths arrived we also got a white Commer van, which would hold about ten of us. Uncle Alan painted it a ghastly green colour, making the van instantly recognisable. Everyone who saw it would say, 'Here come those children from the home.' I was embarrassed whenever I had to ride in it.

This was one misery Uncle Alan caused us inadvertently. Most of the others increasingly seemed to be intentional. Indeed, our honeymoon with the new houseparents was quickly over. As I remember it, as soon as Uncle and Auntie had settled in, and were no longer being scrutinised by the social services, their dispositions deteriorated rapidly.

Uncle Alan would regularly line us up in the dining room, march up and down in front of us and then give us a thorough lecture as to our faults. He would terrify the little ones. He didn't beat them but when he played ball with the children in the back garden, he threw the ball too hard, sometimes narrowly missing them and frightening them. When he wanted to make a point, he stood close to you, putting his nose right up to your face. He did it to some of the staff as well as the children.

One evening, almost as soon as he got home from work – he was a laboratory assistant – he lined us up, marched grumpily back and forth, and said that Auntie Brenda had told him that we had been noisy on our return from school, which had given her a headache. As a punishment we were being sent to bed early. This was unfair. We had been no noisier than usual, and it was something entirely different, something not our fault, which had caused or contributed to her headache. I immediately said so.

Drowning out my protest, Uncle Alan said that I could not go out for a week after school hours as I had answered back.

What had put Auntie Brenda in a foul mood and then given her a headache was a little contretemps she had had with her staff and me about one of her many sins of omission, her two chief ones being that she didn't give us any affection and she didn't give us enough food to eat. It was the latter point that had caused the flare-up that morning. Tired of being hungry and beans, beans, beans, I had complained, only to find that the staff supported me. One of the assistant housemothers, Mrs Peat, a forthright cockney who often spoke her mind, and Edna the cleaner gave Mrs Smith what for, complaining that the food they gave to us children was atrocious and that there was simply not enough of it to fill us up.

Mrs Smith got a headache, but instead of one tin of beans between seven children that day we had two tins of beans between seven. Imagine if we had had a full house of nine or ten.

Nor was this an isolated incident. Mrs Peat, whose job was similar to Cory's, worked at the home thirty hours a week. She and the other thirty-hour ladies often had to purchase food from the shops across the street, using their own money, because there wasn't enough food in the house to make a meal. Eventually they would get reimbursed, but they were not pleased with the situation.

My best friend Alma Riley, whom I had met at school, lived in the children's home around the corner. They always had enough to eat and appeared to be better dressed than us. That home was entirely different from ours. Alma was happy there. And the houseparents would always be kind to me when I called. I was often given a drink and some biscuits.

Alma and I did everything together. We were both in the Brownies and liked sport. I was stronger, but Alma was a faster runner than me, a real sprinter. She had lived in a children's home since her mother died when she was two, and was my friend from the time I started junior school, aged seven. I felt that Alma, who was nine or ten months younger than me, was more my sister than Aliya was. Alma was black. At school there were not many black children, but there was a lot of racial prejudice. As Alma reminded me recently, when other children taunted her with ugly names, I would take it upon myself to beat them up.

My other best friend, Wendy, who was full of fun and cheeky in the nicest possible way, was white and lived in a normal home. Her mum treated me like one of her own, giving me toast and marmalade, and even coffee in the morning when I called in on the way to school, and, if I wanted something – and I usually did – in the afternoon too. I was always very hungry, partly because I was always expending energy – running across the school playground, or illicitly climbing trees – and partly because we just were not fed enough at the home.

Sometimes I would go to Wendy's after school to watch *Jackanory* on television – and eat after-school tea and biscuits and sometimes sandwiches. If not, I sometimes felt, I would have starved. It seemed to me that everyone except the children at our home had plenty to eat and adults who were kind to look after them. But we had to put up with 'Hitler', which is what we privately called Uncle Alan. And Mrs Smith whom we referred to as 'Her'.

Even when I was still very young Uncle and Auntie found me to be among their less tractable charges. They were not overly fond of me. To tell the truth, I don't think they really liked any of us children very much.

They certainly made sure we were not over-privileged. When it came time for the Brownies to go camping, Brown Owl had to have a special word with her to get permission for me to go. The Brownie leader even supplied the two blankets and sheet for my sleeping bag. I will never forget the week we girls had, following trails in the woods, singing around the campfire at night and sleeping under the stars. There wasn't a single day of rain.

One Saturday morning Mrs Smith told me that the woman they called my mother, and whom I thought of as the fat old cow, was coming later that day to take Aliya and me to London to stay with her for the weekend.

I didn't want to go, and said so. But Mrs Smith insisted I had to go, and confined me to quarters, that is the girl's bedroom, to wait. The other girls were playing outdoors. I slumped on my bed, feeling desperately upset.

Aliya poked her head into the room. 'You're not my real sister,' she said. 'My mummy doesn't love you.'

'I hate you,' I shouted. 'I hate the fat old cow. I hate all of you.'

'My mummy doesn't want you. My mummy doesn't want you.' Aliya ran down the stairs. She took great delight in taunting me in this way. She lived with the woman on and off. I never did. No one in the home or at school who hadn't been told would have thought we were sisters. Not even half-sisters. There was no bond, no friendliness, no closeness.

We didn't even look alike and our personalities were completely different. Aliya was puny. She didn't run and play like me so she didn't have my sturdy build. Although I was only eight or nine I already had reasonable muscles. She was listless and quiet, and she usually did what the Smiths told her. She wasn't a fighter like me. Maybe she didn't need to be. She did get a bit depressed sometimes, but her attitude was that she had a family. Mine was that I didn't. I was the only one Aliya ever caused any aggro.

After our little shouting match, I slunk downstairs and pleaded with Mrs Smith not to send me away with that woman. 'It is clear they don't want me,' I said tearfully. 'And I don't want to be with them.' Mrs Smith did not attempt to comfort me. Instead, she seemed pleased that I was going to be away for the weekend, and hurried me off back to the bedroom, where I vented my anger and frustration by muttering 'fat old cow' over and over.

The woman they said was my mother was not that outlandishly fat, but I had to have some name for her. I wouldn't dare call the woman that to her face. In fact, I didn't call her anything. Certainly not mother.

She eventually arrived, late, as usual. I was now resigned to going. It could even, I told myself, be interesting. There were new things to see. There would probably be more than enough to eat. And maybe, maybe, it would be all right. Aliya and I walked down the road from the home with the woman. Aliya was told to take off her glasses and put them in her bag. The woman then took Aliya's hand and talked to her in their language.

I was walking alongside Aliya, and when we reached the crossroads to turn right for the bus, the woman stopped and told me to go back. She said she didn't want me. Then, she took half a crown out of her purse and gave it to me. At first I thought she must be joking and that as I started to walk back towards the home she would call out to me. But she didn't. It was no joke. I wondered why she had changed her mind. I hadn't been naughty. I hadn't had time to be. Although originally I had not wanted to go with her, I now felt completely empty.

By the time I reached the home, not only did I feel alone in the whole world, but ashamed and embarrassed that I had to tell Mrs Smith that the woman didn't want me. When I opened the back door, Mrs Smith was shouting at one of the younger children. She stopped to ask me if I had forgotten something. Between sobs, I blurted out what had happened. I was crying out to be comforted. Mrs Smith showed no feelings and offered me no comfort. All she said was, 'Well you didn't want to go anyway.'

Feeling totally rejected by everyone I went to the girls' bedroom, where I sat staring at the walls. My hatred for the fat woman was now complete. I was determined never to call her my mum.

In retrospect, it is still hard to follow her reasoning that day. I can only imagine that she had never wanted or intended to take me for the weekend, but that the social worker had insisted. It was easier for her to tell me 'no' than to tell someone in authority. So, the woman simply waited until no one connected with the social services was about, and then she sent me back. She gave me the half a crown to sweeten the blow. She knew it was a blow.

After that episode, I began to withdraw even more into myself and started to build a wall around me. Outwardly I became much more aggressive and tougher. I gave Mrs Smith plenty of reason to wish I would disappear for the weekend. I kept asking myself what I had done to deserve what was happening to me. I felt in a turmoil and became obsessed with the fact that no one wanted me. There didn't seem to be any hope. I was well on the way to a breakdown.

I was old enough to realise that all of us were disadvantaged children. But I asked myself why the two people we called Auntie and Uncle seemed to have no feelings for us. Mrs Smith had not comforted me during my hours of need. Nor did I feel she offered understanding or sympathy at any time. Although when a social worker visited the home Mrs Smith would sit one of the young children on her knee.

Myself, I had very few visits from social workers, and little solace from them. They didn't know me well enough to be much help. They had too many cases. They couldn't be expected to concentrate on mine. But one wet summer afternoon, a new woman social worker came to the house to see me. She told me that she had traced my father.

5

The Visit

The man and woman arrived in a big, pink car. It was an amazing car, an old-style Jaguar, with great, long, undulating bumpers. The woman was driving because the man they said was my daddy couldn't drive and it was her car. He had thick, wavy hair, dark like mine, flopping over his forehead, and a foreign accent. When he got out of the pink car, the man gave me a big bag of sweets. The woman, whose name was Pamela, had long, straight hair and was thin and very pretty. She called him Michael.

Mrs Smith served cups of tea to the two of them in the lounge. Whilst he was drinking his tea, the man asked me to sit on his lap. I eagerly climbed up.

'Do you want to come home with me on a visit?' He ruffled my hair. I liked sitting on his lap.

'Yes, please.' My clothes were already packed. School was out for the summer and the social worker had long since told me that I was going to be staying with him for a week. Michael and Pamela and even Mrs Smith seemed as delighted as I was at the prospect. And Mrs Smith was actually nice.

Although I was excited as we left in that wonderful car, I was also just a little apprehensive. Leaving the home even for a visit was, in effect, leaving behind all my security. But although I was in the back seat, which Pamela said was safer, I enjoyed the journey.

However, London was a shock. It was so dirty. Michael lived in a flat on the first floor of a large old house in a run-down part of Stamford Hill in North London. There were not many trees on the street, but there certainly was a lot of rubbish, and not just on that road – all over London. I couldn't understand why the whole

43

world didn't come to Essex to live. It was neater, tidier and cleaner, and there were trees to climb.

Nor did people bump into you on the street or push waiting for the bus, as they did the next morning as Michael and I were queuing at the bus-stop. As we sat hunched together on the red bus, he confided, 'You will see, little one, three barbers work for me. I come from Cyprus with almost nothing. But in my fingers I have the first ingredient of success, a trade.' He held his right hand in front of us like an item of evidence to be examined in a trial. His fingers were blunt and well manicured, and there was a scattering of dark hair on the back of his hand.

'The second ingredient, little one, is inside here.' He touched his head. 'But hard work, little one, that is the essential ingredient of success. You remember that.'

I nodded.

'Good girl. Any honest trade is respectable. Even to work in a taverna or in a cafe.' He smiled, his white teeth glittering like a string of taverna lights. We got off the bus and on to another on which we stayed until we got to a big cinema. The shop was very nearby. It was a pity that Michael couldn't drive because every day he had to catch two different buses and leave early in the morning to get there on time. We had not had enough time for breakfast, and when we got to the shop, he sat me down with a big bowl of cereal, and began preparing for the customers.

Wolfing down breakfast so that I would be allowed to help, I carefully placed the towels in position, making sure they were folded, not rumpled. Michael and the three other barbers cleaned the mirrors and the razors which were really clean already, as they had been done the night before. The other barbers were all foreign too, but very friendly. One spoke good English, but it was not as good as Michael's. Michael had an accent, but he was fluent.

To set me up for the morning, we went to buy some sweets and a bottle of cherryade which was my favourite drink. Then the customers started coming in. They were all shapes and sizes, even bald ones who came for a shave.

I spent most of the day sitting in a dirty little backroom which had a small table with a chair and a small sink. I often looked round

The Visit

the corner of the door to see what was happening in the shop and the customers would wave to me. They would smile as they walked through the tiny room to go to the toilet which was in the yard outside. But they said very little for most of them spoke a foreign language.

One afternoon when there were no customers in the barber shop, Michael put a wooden board across the arms of the chair and lifted me up on to it. As I sat on the board looking in the mirror, he tucked a huge white barbers' sheet under my neck and draped it over my shoulders, exactly the way he draped it over the customers. But I was entirely covered; even my toes. Then he went to the back of the shop to get some special scissors. As I waited, I felt very important.

'Now, little one, I will make you a beautiful haircut.' He ran his thumb lightly over one of the scissor blades. 'These scissors are very fine quality.'

He looked pleased with himself. I was beaming too, even though he hadn't yet clipped a single lock. His hair was black like mine. His hair was wavy like mine. He had a short, very neatly cropped haircut. I wanted one exactly like that.

'Like yours,' I said, twisting around in my seat and reaching out to touch his head. From my high perch I was able to reach it. His hair was soft but springy.

'Sit up, you must sit straight,' he said a little gruffly. 'I'm cutting.' He began to cut my hair, snip, snip, snip. 'Keep your head still.' He was concentrating. As the locks of my hair fell on to the barbers' sheet or on to the floor, I watched in the mirror with rapt attention.

'There,' he said at last. 'You like?'

He had cut my hair short but not as short as his. A little bob. I loved it.

He let me sweep the hair off the floor of the shop. This gave me infinite pleasure. You hold on to the good things. I will never forget the joy I felt at looking at my new hairstyle, and knowing he had made it. As I swept the hair away, I felt almost as though I was sweeping away the loneliness of my previous life. On the way home this man whom I had been told was my daddy bought

45

me some more sweets, bags full, including my favourites which were Smarties, and another bottle of cherryade. The next evening he bought me some shoes. They were little boy's shoes.

As the week wore on, I think I became a burden. On one of the afternoons I was taken round to the nearby cinema by Michael who bought me some popcorn and left me to watch the film, as he had arranged with one of the usherettes to send me back to the shop when the show was over.

That evening, when we returned to his flat, an elderly woman who couldn't speak any English, and two younger women were there eating a meal. They were Michael's mother and two sisters. The elderly woman gave us each a portion of rice and meat, and the man ate some of the black, garlicky olives and a few other hot, spicy foods which I did not recognise. In deference to my British palate, the old lady had cooked me a portion that wasn't spicy.

I think they had lived in Britain for a long time, even though the elderly woman couldn't speak any English. Her clothes were entirely westernised, as were her daughters'. The family talked a lot over the meal, gesticulating lavishly and laughing, but they spoke to each other only in the foreign language. I felt homesick for the children's home because I could not understand what was being said.

During the meal, because of something one of his sisters said, the man flew into a rage, throwing food across the room. It went everywhere. He was shouting in that strange language and stormed out. I was very frightened and began to cry. The three women tried to comfort me but could not calm me down as I was so nervous and frightened.

Later that evening the man returned. I was relieved to see him, and stuck to him like glue until I fell asleep. I woke up as his mother and sisters were leaving, and was afraid he was leaving too. After they had gone, I would not let him put me to bed anywhere but beside him on the huge converted sofa. Later that night his girlfriend Pamela arrived at the flat and he took me to a little bedroom which was very cold and put me under the covers. When he told me to stay there, I did not protest this time because there was an angry edge to his voice and anyway I was three-quarters asleep.

When I woke in the morning I ran to the other room to find it empty. The man and the woman had both gone. I ran upstairs to the flat above where the woman told me he had asked her to look after me as he couldn't take me to work. She told me to get dressed and to go outside and play with the children in the street. The day seemed so long and I began to feel so lonely that I wanted to go back to the home.

The lady who was supposed to be looking after me took me to the shops and I kept asking her when was my daddy coming home. She would only tell me, 'Later'. When he finally came I stuck to him so closely I probably got on his nerves. I was scared he was going to leave me.

He took me to the sweet shop and on the way back, just as I was beginning to feel very happy and contented again, he told me I had to go back to the children's home. I started to cry and he then told me not to worry as he would collect me again the following weekend.

That night, as I settled down to sleep beside him, Pamela arrived and I was taken to the other room where I lay feeling completely rejected. After a while I decided to go back and join them, but when I got there they were arguing. He was shouting and Pamela was crying. When I heard my name, I listened at the door.

'But, Michael, now that you have Fatima, it doesn't matter anymore that I can't have any children.'

'It isn't enough for me.'

'But she's lovely. She even looks like you, Michael.'

'I say no. No, no, no.'

Pamela was in love with him. She wanted to marry him. She wanted me. But he wanted to live in a normal happy family with the mother of his child, his children. He wanted to watch his baby grow up. Who could blame him? He wanted a typical family, he said. He wanted what other men had. He wanted a son.

The next morning when we went back to the children's home in the car, Pamela had dark rings under her eyes and Michael looked tired and rumpled. They had spent most of the night arguing. Although I was feeling miserable, I was consoled by the fact that I was going to come back again next weekend.

At the home, Michael did not come in but left me with Mrs Smith at the door. As he left, my feelings welled up and I began crying. I was heartbroken. I cried for a long time, but again Mrs Smith showed no understanding or sympathy and sent me to the bedroom where I spent most of the day on my own. Mrs Smith told me to grow up and not to be silly. What I was crying out for was a hug, but instead I was sent upstairs to sort things out for myself. Occasionally one of the other children came in to stare at me. I would tell them to go away.

During the next few days, to feel closer to him, I kept with me the few things that Michael had given me – the shoes and the empty cherryade bottle. Throughout that week I waited for a telephone call to say that he was coming to collect me. But if he rang, Mrs Smith did not tell me.

At the weekend I waited hour after hour for him to arrive and at the sound of every car I rushed to the window. The weather was fine on Sunday afternoon, and I sat on the front wall of the house waiting. Mrs Smith told me she didn't know whether or not he was coming. When he didn't, she offered me no consolation.

He didn't come the next week either.

Weekend after weekend, feeling more and more rejected and desperate, I waited for the man I had been told was my daddy. I wanted so much not to be let down again and to be wanted. Most of the children were so disturbed themselves that they did not notice what was happening to me. Only Sham, who was a few years older than me – he was the oldest boy at the home – teased me. He never missed a chance of upsetting anyone. 'Your Dad is not ever coming to see you,' he said.

'He is too.'

'If he was coming, he would come, wouldn't he,' said Sham with irrefutable logic.

'He is. You'll see,' I said. I stalked off.

I shut myself in the bathroom. To hide the sound of my sobbing and my wails of frustration, I turned on the water. Sham was right, of course. Michael wasn't coming.

There were constant changes among the children at the home, with some returning to their parents and others becoming fostered by families. Aliya continued to come and go between the home and her mother. No one, however, seemed to want me. I felt utter despair. It was a feeling I had felt before, all too often, a feeling that all of us children in the home knew well.

He never came to see me again. But as much as that hurt, I am now grateful that he didn't keep worrying the situation, building my hopes and smashing them again. He had tried, probably partly for Pamela's sake. He had even got his mother and sisters involved, but it hadn't worked. He didn't feel he could bring me up so he cut the emotional umbilical cord. He had made his decision and that was it. I try to think it was a case of being cruel to be kind.

A few years later the woman who said she was my mother took me to Michael's shop in Stamford Hill and sent me in to cadge some money from 'my father'. Reluctantly, and with embarrassment, I poked my head into the barber's where, as I remember it, he was in the middle of cutting a customer's hair. None the less, Michael did give me some money. I don't remember how much because the woman or Adem immediately took it off me.

Then I completely lost track of Michael. When I tried to find the shop not that long ago, it wasn't there, although I did locate what I think was the nearby cinema. Sad to say, the man who sowed the seed that gave birth to me is a stranger – although he did get in touch one day when I was beginning to make a name for myself as an athlete, but was struggling to make ends meet. Michael made me an offer many people would find hard to refuse. He told me that he was now well off – indeed rich, a millionaire – and he offered to be my sponsor. I was grateful for the offer. But it was guilt-money. I couldn't take it. By then I was a very different person from the forlorn little girl who needed an emotional umbilical cord, who so desperately needed to be loved. I will never forget how bereft I felt when he failed to reappear at the home.

6

Auntie Rae

I began to become very attached to the 'thirty-hour lady', Mrs Peat, who, I am convinced, kept me sane.

Rachel, 'Rae', Whitney Peat, a sturdy reed of a woman in her forties, was the embodiment of cockney grit. Snub-nosed with fair crinkly hair and boundless energy, she had come to Essex fifteen years earlier with her husband Joe, who had a good job at Ford's in Dagenham. After raising her two sons in a house around the corner from the home, Rae Peat took a job there looking after the unblest children other people had cast off. Not everything at the home pleased her, and as she didn't really have to work, and cared deeply, she felt at liberty to say so.

She had been at the home almost as long as I had. We children called her Auntie Rae. Auntie Rae had very soft hands. She was always rubbing Oil of Ulay into the palms of her hands, and when she did the dusting, she wore gloves.

When she was on early shift, which began at seven a.m., Auntie Rae's first task of the day was to wake us children up. 'Wakey, wakey, rise and shine, another day has begun,' she would chant. Most of the children would jump out of bed, smiling. Not me. I pretended to be asleep, so that she would have to come and squeeze my shoulder. Out of the corner of my eye, I would just catch sight of her pale blue overall but I would lie very still. Then she would tickle me. And as hard as I tried, I could not hold out. I would burst out laughing.

After beginning the day with a giggle, I would not have much time to wallow in my sorrows, since I had to rush off to school. If I or any of the others had wet the bed, Auntie Rae would brush

50

over the incident, whereas it seemed to me that Mrs Smith acted as if we had done it on purpose. In my opinion, Auntie Rae should have been matron. She cared about us children and she took a lot of responsibilities home, even though, like all the 'thirty-hour ladies' at the home, she was only supposed to work and only paid for thirty hours a week.

But it never was just thirty hours. When Auntie Rae was on an early shift, some little thing would usually keep her an hour or more later than the usual time to go home, which was supposedly one p.m. She was not paid any overtime, of course. The late shift, which included putting us to bed, started at four p.m. and was supposed to finish at seven p.m. but she would be lucky to get home at a quarter to nine – and her house was only three minutes walk from the children's home. Her husband Joe would grumble, but he cooked their evening meal if she was late.

Her house was on my route home from school. On the days when I knew her shift at the children's home had ended for the day, or if it was her week off, as I passed her house, I would wonder what Auntie was doing. I tried to imagine her putting her feet up, or preparing the evening meal for her son and her husband, or doing whatever it was you did in your own house.

One afternoon when I was, as usual, fed up with the home, with school, with my life, I slowed down to a snail's pace, and then paused in front of Auntie Rae's little red-brick house. I could see her standing at the kitchen sink under the big window, doing the washing up. Auntie Rae liked everything to be neat and tidy and clean, just so. She was so engrossed in her task that she didn't notice me. I knocked, tentatively, at her door.

Auntie Rae welcomed me with a hug and a big smacking kiss on the cheek, and sat me down at her oiled teak kitchen table, which is as unmarked today as it was then, to serve me biscuits and tea. Auntie Rae placed my mug of tea on the table mat in front of me. The mat was a delicate colour, fawn. There was nice bright orange, beige, and gold flowered wallpaper on the top half of the kitchen wall. The bottom half was clean paint-work.

As I dangled my short legs from her comfortable kitchen chair,

51

waiting for my tea to cool enough to drink, I said plaintively, 'It's not fair that I have to live in the home.'

'Life isn't always fair, Fatima.'

'But my life is horrible. I feel miserable.' Actually, this wasn't, at the moment, quite true. I was enjoying our tea party immensely. I was especially enjoying being in Auntie Rae's kitchen. Being the centre of attention was nice too. But, since in principle it was perfectly true that I was miserable, I continued to whine. 'I'm tired of Uncle Alan saying, "Fatima, stop this, and, Fatima, stop that." And *she* is always getting at me. I hate my life. I don't know what to do, Auntie Rae.'

'Have a biscuit.'

While I was chewing it, and beginning to feel quite contented, Auntie Rae said, 'Remember this. Everything comes to those who wait.'

'I don't see why I should wait for what other children already have.'

'Just you remember,' Auntie Rae said gently. 'Now off you go, Fats (that was short for Fatima) or you will be late, and Mrs Smith will give you what for.'

But I took a moment for a little look round before leaving. In the lounge, there were snapshots of her grandchildren on the wall.

'Fatima, you don't have to memorise the place,' she said. She gave me to understand I could stop in for a cuppa whenever.

And one Saturday, she invited me to go shopping with her. We went from shop to shop, and everywhere I looked, I saw other children holding on to their mother's hands. 'Can I hold your hand?'

'You're getting to be a bit big for that, Fatima.'

I put my hand in my mouth and began to suck my fingers. It was a little habit I had. Auntie Rae noticed. 'Your fingers will get distorted if you keep that up.' She took my hand in hers.

I liked walking hand in hand like that. 'Can I call you Mummy, too?'

'Fatima, I'm not your mummy. I'm your Auntie Rae.'

'But can I call you Mummy, just for today?'

'Just for today. There is no harm in that.'

'Mummy,' I said.

'Yes?'

'Just Mummy.'

On her birthday, I sneaked into the neighbour's garden and picked a huge bunch of bright yellow daffodils for her. She had so many flowers, especially daffs, growing in her own garden, that I knew she must really like them. Taking the note I had painstakingly printed letter by letter in my own childish hand, I went to deliver them. I had to do a stealthy recce first, creeping around the corner to her front gate, and only when I was absolutely certain that Auntie Rae was not standing at the sink and looking out of the big window, did I tiptoe up to her kitchen door, and lay the daffs and my note on her doorstep. Then I knocked loudly, and ran off.

Perhaps it was a good thing that I was not there when she opened the note and read: 'Dear Auntie Rae, Will you please be my mum?'

The next day, Auntie Rae explained to me very carefully that she could not be my mum but that she cared about me and would look after me whenever she could. She had her own family, she reminded me – children as well as the grandchildren. Her eldest son Mick taught at my primary school. Her other son, Chris, was a lot younger. But since she was at the home so much of the time, and I was always welcome for tea at her house, we would be seeing each other, she pointed out, almost as much as a mum and daughter did.

But whenever I was on a jaunt with her, or visiting her house – I now went almost every day after school – I pretended Auntie Rae was my mother and that the children's home didn't exist. Then walking back from her house to the home, the truth would hit me. I was alone in the world.

When Auntie Rae paid attention to other children in the home I would feel upset, as I wanted her to pay special attention just to me. As always, I wanted to be special, special to someone, to be wanted, to have a mum.

On her doorstep I left some more daffs and a handful of the neighbour's bright blue irises, along with this note:

To My – – –
And here is a gift
Love
Fats

'Fatima,' Auntie Rae said one morning, 'please come and help me. Shay here needs looking after. Give her a big kiss for me.' Shay was a little Nigerian girl, three years younger than I was, and very disturbed. She was banging her head against the wall. When she was in bed, Shay would often hit her head, bang, bang, bang against the wall, and if she was sitting on the bed or in a chair, she would rock. I went over to her and put my arm around her.

'Where is my daddy?' she said. 'Want my daddy.'

'He'll come along when he can, Shay. Come out to the garden now and play.'

'Want my daddy.'

'He'll come when he can,' I repeated. 'Everything comes to those who wait.' I gave Shay a big smacker of a kiss on the cheek, just like Auntie Rae would have, and trundled her out to the garden. She began to play with the other children and forgot about her woes.

Auntie Rae was very pleased with me. 'These children need you,' she said. 'You're getting to be a big girl. The little children look to you and need the comfort you can give them.'

I had never thought of being needed before, only of being needy. Now, for the first time, I began to realise that the other children needed to be loved too. Many of them were as starved emotionally as I was. Shay was one of the worst, but Verlie used to cry all the time, too, because she wanted to go home. Her mum couldn't care for her because she had had a nervous breakdown. It was not her mum's first breakdown either. I went home with Verlie for the day once, and her dad did everything because his wife couldn't get out of bed. She was too ill. Verlie cried all the way back to the home, and her father, who was driving us, was annoyed.

Rakash, one of the Indian boys at the home, was teased mercilessly by his older brother Sham, who I regarded as a nasty

54

piece of work. Sham would chase him round the dining room table, and Rakash would get into a state. He would be crying and scared. But whenever I tried to make Sham leave Rakash alone, Rakash would turn on me and defend his brother. In retrospect it is touching; it wasn't at the time. I would get peeved.

I was entirely unsympathetic to Sham. I regarded him as a dangerous sneak and didn't at all like the way he made up to the Smiths to get extra privileges. But I suppose Sham wasn't happy either. He, like me, was a bit of a veteran.

Helping Auntie Rae look after the other children was, in fact, very satisfying. And Auntie Rae encouraged me. 'When I'm not here,' she said, 'I want you to make sure the children are all right. I want you to take over where I leave off.'

Now, instead of being jealous that she cared about the other boys and girls, I felt pleased and very proud that she was entrusting them to me. When Auntie Rae's shift was over, and she went home for the day, I would try hard to carry on where she had left off. And for the first time in my life, through the children, I began to feel needed, which is very close to feeling wanted.

By now, I was no longer one of the little ones. I was getting on for ten. I became the big sister even to children my own age. 'You're just like a little mum,' Auntie Rae said one day. I was thrilled. But she was such a clever 'child psychologist' that I never once realised what she had been up to. Auntie Rae understood more about children, and cared more than many far better educated people. She had a talent for understanding us.

Auntie Rae was the person who most shaped me from the age of seven or eight through early adolescence. Those were a crucial half dozen years, and I owe what went right about them to her. She taught me character. That was the most important thing in life. I learnt that you gave as well as took, that you did not steal or cheat and you tried not to lie, but you could fib a little if people deserved it. I also learnt that you worked for a living because work gave you self-respect, and you worked hard. You tried to put aside a quid or two for a rainy day but you always had plenty of laughter and you could not have too much of that. But there was no harm either in being serious at serious moments or in telling unpopular truths. And being the best you could be at whatever you did was something to be proud of.

Auntie Rae had a lot of love in her heart. Enough to teach me — by a combination of example and gentle prodding – that love was not just wanting someone, it was giving too. I now prided myself on being almost a mother to the younger ones.

To cheer up bedtime, which was one of the worst times at this home, just as it had been at Wormley Hill, I invented Rosie Row. I would tell stories about Rosie's many escapades, always whispering, of course, so we wouldn't have Mrs Smith shouting at us. Auntie Brenda's voice seemed only to operate at a screech or a shout. Under the Smiths' regime, as in the previous one, bedwetters were required to stay awake for a late visit to the toilet. Rosie Row helped keep them awake, so that Mrs Smith, who was no gentler than the previous matron, would not have to shake them so roughly.

Rosie Row was a very special sort of rabbit. Rosie had big pointed ears and a soft, furry, pink chest — that's why she or he (I never said which because Rosie was just a rabbit) was called Rosie. Now this rabbit, who lived in the bottom of a big tree in the forest, used to go round and play with all the other animals. The squirrel was Rosie's friend. And the birds were her friends. Rosie Row was happy. One day when Rosie Row came out of the hole in the bottom of the tree, the squirrel dropped a nut that hit Rosie on the head, and they had a little quarrel. But they got over it. Most of the time there was no trouble in the forest. Rosie Row had tea parties with all the other animals. They would go dancing too, and then it would get very late, and Rosie Row had to scamper home all the way across the forest so that Mummy and Daddy would not be worried that Rosie Row had been killed or gone missing.

If the Smiths treated any of the children unfairly, and in my view, they often did, I would speak out, which made me very unpopular with them. What I called defending the little ones, Uncle Alan called answering back.

There were two main punishments at the home, and often as not, I got both for a single offence. The main punishment for all of us was to have our pocket money stopped. It wasn't a fortune to begin with, but I often wondered what happened to the pocket money we children didn't get.

I particularly remember one time when Uncle Alan had been bawling out some of the little children for no good reason, and really frightening them. I told him that it was not on. He got very cross. 'Who do you think you are, their mother?' he said.

I not only lost my pocket money that week, but he delivered the *coup de grâce* — I was not to be allowed to go out of the house for a week except to go to school. That meant that I could not visit Auntie Rae on the way home from school. He knew that I lived to visit Auntie Rae.

There was no way around the punishment. I could not even go into the garden. I didn't know how I would get through a whole week when I was not only deprived of our visits, but I couldn't even play outdoors to work off my pent-up frustration. No running, no jumping, no hide and seek. 'I have to rot indoors,' I told Auntie Rae bitterly.

'Just wait it out,' she said. 'Try not to let it upset you. A week will soon pass.'

That week seemed like 20,000 decades to me. The only place I was allowed to go, thank you very much, was to school. School, was not my favourite venue. I don't suppose I was the easiest of pupils either. That week, I had tons of resentment welling up inside me, and at school I was even worse than usual. Not that I was ordinarily *that* bad, but at junior school I was one of the toughies.

There was a set of us, ten- and eleven-year-olds, who clubbed together. Wendy, my friend whose mum made such good sandwiches, and Alma, who lived at the home around the corner, were in our set; and Keith who was my boyfriend. He was a very tough little kid, even smaller than me. Now he is much taller than I am. During playtime, the teachers could usually find us all at the back of the school, out of bounds. That is, until we discovered a way to disappear.

Because we were the littlest, Keith or I used to climb into the school through a small window, open the fire door, and steal into the library where there was a TV. Nobody used the room at lunchtime, and we would sit undisturbed watching the telly and smoking the odd cigarette. But if the dinner ladies did come round, we would hide and shut the door. They never found us. They probably didn't want to.

In class, all of us were cheeky, making jokes during lessons, that sort of thing. I saw no reason not to. Most of what was on offer was a joke anyway, but I could see a reason for learning maths – for starters, you needed to be able to count your money when you went to the shops. To be honest, though, the main reason I learned my multiplication tables speedily was that you got a gold star pasted beside your name on the chart every time you learnt a new one. I always tried to have more stars than anyone else. Later on I could see a practical reason for learning how to compute circumferences and all that, even equations. I took that fairly seriously.

But learning the capitals of countries I had never heard of meant nothing to me. And reading was far less interesting to me than running. I said so too – in a jokey way. Being boisterous was preferable to being bored.

I was often called in to see the headmaster, for some infraction or other. Actually, it wasn't his fault. It was mine. I had boundless energy. I admit that I was a bit of a villain, not a wicked one, not a thief or anything like that, but I knew how to be a pest. I didn't see any reason not to be. The world was not fair, why play by the rules?

The school dinners were a horrible reminder that children from the home were different from the rest because you had to show a pink chit to get your meal. Nowadays, at a school with 1,000 pupils, 900 would probably get free lunches, 50 would pay, and 50 would go home to eat. But when I was at school the situation was different. Your life had to be wretched to qualify for free lunch, and everybody knew it. You either lived in a children's home or were otherwise dead poor. So there was a stigma attached. There were only fifty or fewer of us free-lunch kids.

I would often skip lunch to avoid the embarrassment of lining up for the chittie in front of the other children. This is part of the reason I always had such a good appetite when I arrived at Wendy's house or at Auntie Rae's.

On the other hand, on those occasions when I was so hungry that I did condescend to eat the school meal, you always knew I was there. I was one of those who would flick peas around the room off the end of a knife. And I would always push to the front of the queue so that if any second helpings were available I was ready with an empty plate. I didn't want anybody to think I was embarrassed about anything.

What saved me from becoming a rebel without a cause was sport. I was beginning to realise I was good at it. When I was ten and in my last year at junior school, we had to throw a cricket ball, and I out-threw every single boy in the school. I threw a long way too, about 50 metres which was good for that age. If you consider that there were about 300 students at the school, of which at least half were boys, that added up to 150 boys. My status at school rose rapidly – in the eyes of all the girls and most of the boys, although there were a few who were rather scathing. I am lucky I was ten years old instead of in my teens, or I might have worried more about having the good opinion of those boys.

What I didn't know then was that bowling in cricket has a lot in common with throwing a javelin. There is much the same whiplash motion.

Actually, I don't remember the ins and outs of that cricket competition except that every year throwing the cricket ball was an event during track and field day. Cricket was not particularly a great love of mine, although I had already begun to realise that the sports fields were my natural habitat. What mattered to me was that I had gone out there and thrown the ball myself, and no one had helped me, and when it was over, the whole school knew and was buzzing about my achievement.

One thing was crystal clear. I might not have as good clothes as some children, or as much spending money, or parents; I might be disadvantaged in every way – no, correction, I *definitely* was disadvantaged in every way – except one. Sport.

There, it was becoming more and more apparent, I was anybody's equal. I always felt happy kicking the ball around. I would play football with the boys, but only because there were not any girls who wanted to play. I was no wimp at rounders either. Nor, by the way, was I too terrible at 'penny up the wall', which I would play with the toughies among the boys somewhere at the back of the school, usually out of bounds. We played for money, of course. My winnings, which were substantial – often as much as two shillings at a time – were squandered on sweets.

At school, PE was my best subject by far. When I threw a ball, or kicked it, the ball went close to where I aimed it. It was almost effortless. (Of course in those days, I wasn't trying to throw anything well over 250 feet.) One of the teachers even told me – and she must have meant it because she was angry with me at the time – that sport was my saving grace.

Auntie Rae said I was a bit of a tomboy, but she didn't seem to see anything really wrong in it, and I certainly didn't. I was one of the best marbles players in the school too. Running and jumping and throwing, all those activities of sports play, made my body feel good. And I was steadily getting stronger. It was such an entirely new experience to be better than everyone at something that it is no wonder I began to get hooked. Fortunately, the school encouraged sport, including girls' sport. If they had not believed in competition on the athletics field, I dare not think what might have become of me.

It is not bragging outrageously to say I was the star of the school netball team, which was of high calibre. But there were so many good players in that team that I was a little surprised and very, very pleased when the other team members voted me their captain. All seven of us became very close. My friend Wendy was in the team.

The teacher in charge was a serious young woman in her twenties, with dark, wayward hair. She could never quite keep her hair in place, but she had no trouble at all controlling the seven of us. And believe me that was a feat. Her secret was this: she was passionate about netball, and she communicated that passion to us. That is what made her a great sports teacher. But let me dignify that to coach. I no longer remember her name, but I will never forget what she did for me.

She loved her job so she had no trouble keeping practice interesting and keeping us inspired. For once, I didn't play up. I took the game seriously. We all did, and by mid season it looked as though we had a fair chance of winning the District Schools Championship. A month before the final we knew we had a good chance of winning the title.

Then one lunchtime I threw a snowball at one of the dinner ladies who was a real stickler for discipline. The snowball didn't get much of a lift, but it landed smack on target – one of my most successful throws ever. The dinner lady wasn't hurt but her dignity was. As a punishment, I was banned from the netball team.

But there was demonstration at school, a pint-sized 'political' demo spearheaded by the rest of the netball team. Remember, at the time demos were a way of life and had been since the grown-up student revolutions of 1968. At our demo the netball team announced just one non-negotiable demand. They wanted me back on the team. If I wasn't on the team, they wouldn't play. This would mean that the school might as well kiss goodbye to the league title. A petition went around the school asking for me to be reinstated.

The headmaster was a decent sort. But he couldn't rescind the ban just like that. He called me into his office, and after extracting the promise that I wouldn't be doing any more throwing except during PE, he said I could rejoin the team – eventually – and in time for the league final. But on one condition: I had to give my school work a little more effort.

The headmaster knew how to motivate me to work hard in lessons, but he obviously didn't know anything about winning a championship. You couldn't just go out there and play without practising, no matter how good you were. If we took our netball very seriously, so did the other schools. The standard was high. But until I was officially back on the team, I wasn't even eligible to go to practice.

This problem required a little ingenuity. I persuaded the team to practise together at breaktime. During the three weeks I was banned, we had these bootleg practices whenever it was possible, and since we were keen, it was often possible. The headmaster looked the other way. So did our teacher.

By the time I was reinstated, just a week before the final, we felt that we could have taken on Arsenal if they played netball. That is, until the very day of the final. Then, like the others, I was all nerves. I was sucking my fingers when I got into the minibus, and twenty minutes later, when we arrived at Lansdowne School in Thurrock, where our opponents were waiting, I still had my hand in my mouth.

Waiting for the starting whistle, as I stood on the court in my red shirt and navy gym knickers, I almost would have preferred to be playing against Arsenal. They would have been gentler. Lansdowne would have pulled our hair if they could have got away with it. They were as tough a school team as we were, aggressive and, if anything, more rabidly determined. But we were more practised. To be honest, it wasn't entirely a game of skills. I and the rest of our girls did whatever was necessary to win. If the referee was looking elsewhere, we shoved a little, we fouled a little. We shouted at our opponents. Mind you, they did the same. But we won. We were the champions.

I was exhausted at the end of that match, but I also felt elated. I will never ever forget how happy I felt. Back at school, we were hailed as heroines. When we were presented to the school at morning assembly, there was thunderous applause. In front of the entire school, each girl on the team was presented with a small medal. I will never forget the thrill I felt when they handed me mine. It was just a tiny little thing, not much bigger than a two pence piece. It came in a little see-through plastic case. The metal, which had a ball and a netball post stamped on it, was silvery in colour, but it wasn't silver. It wasn't a precious metal at all, but it was my first, a precious medal, precious to me. I had no idea it was to be the first of a long line.

That day at school was glorious. Even the dinner ladies were nice to me and seemed genuinely glad to see me – that was a change. But I couldn't wait for the school day to be over. When the final bell rang, I rushed out of the building, ran down the steps and hurried to Auntie Rae's, running most of the way. When she opened the door, I threw myself in her arms. 'I got the medal,' I exclaimed. 'Look.'

If anyone was prouder and more pleased than I was, it was Auntie Rae. When I proffered my little medal as though it were the most spectacular of the Crown Jewels, Auntie Rae looked with rapt attention and hugged me again. It was a jubilant moment.

Then I surprised both Auntie Rae and myself. I gave my medal to her, and she still has it to this day. At first she wouldn't take it, but when I insisted, she said she would treasure it. Over the years, she has offered to give it back to me many times, but I get great pleasure from knowing that it is there.

The adulation I received as the star and captain of the netball team made me feel I was wanted at last. No wonder sport was getting under my skin. What I found was that I could lose myself in any sports activity. Paradoxically, I was at the very same time finding my true self in sport. And I had adored my first whiff of the sweet smell of success. For the first time in my life, I had a place in the world.

Not long after, when I returned from school one afternoon, Aliya's social worker was there. Aliya had been on a lengthy visit to her mother. I think it was for some months. The social worker, who had just brought her back to the home, asked me to go upstairs to see her in the bedroom.

Aliya was unpacking her clothes and putting them in the locker beside her bed. She was crying. The woman they said was my mother was there too. Suddenly she grabbed me by the throat and told me that unless I looked after Aliya she would cut my throat. I was very frightened. Then in her broken English she said it twice more. 'I cut your throat, I cut your throat.' She probably didn't mean it literally but I was terrified.

I was now nearly eleven, and in the last year at junior school. Towards the end of the term, our class went as a group to visit Culverhouse Comprehensive which was the school we were to start after the summer break. It was a twenty-minute walk away, on the other side of a huge housing estate. None the less, the school looked all right to me until the deputy head, Miss Meredith, came up to me and said, 'We know all about you, Fatima. We're ready for you. You'd better watch your step when you get here.'

Her remark really upset me. I was by no means the worse troublemaker at junior school and I was still naughty, not nasty. I had had no idea until then that I had an unsavoury reputation, especially one that went beyond the walls of the school. That remark made me feel that I wouldn't get a fair chance and that no matter where I went nobody wanted me. Auntie Rae did her best to console me.

Soon after, the Smiths took us children in the green van to Rhyl in Wales for the summer holiday. The van was not comfortable at the best of times, and this was one of the worst drives. It was like a typical school outing, with plenty of squabbling in the back seats, and singsongs to while away the time. We must have sung the Beatles' songs *Yellow Submarine* and *Lily the Pink* a thousand times. We checked into a decrepit boarding house, where we were sleeping too many to a room, and then were free to wander along the sea front.

One of the cafes in Rhyl, a bustling place overlooking the sea was seeking temporary help. The notice in the window said you would be paid your wages at the end of every day. They wanted girls to clear away dishes and help out in general, carrying meals to the tables and washing up. It was not a glamorous job, but as I was always short of money, I decided I was getting bored just being on holiday.

Mrs Smith encouraged me to take the job. At the end of the first day, the owner told me I would have to wait another day for my pay. After I worked the next day, he said the same. I told him I was not coming back to work as a slave in a packed cafe for no pay.

I was not the only one who quit either. It turned out that he had quite a good thing going. When he hired you, he always said he would pay at the end of each day's work. Then he didn't. And he kept the job notice in the window. After two or three days, the youngsters who were working for him would twig, and walk out. In the end he didn't pay anybody. The experience made me a little leery of the ordinary work-a-day world, where obviously it was so easy to be taken advantage of.

Soon after we returned from Rhyl, I started secondary school. Walking on my own to school the first day, I felt as dour and dreary as my new school uniform, with its lengthy black skirt and dull grey jumper. Passing the big run-down council estate where I knew no one and no one knew me, I felt apprehensive and insignificant.

Outside the school there were hordes of pupils. Culverhouse had over a thousand of them, most of whom I didn't know, and who didn't know me, or appear to want to. I didn't like the look of them either. As I waited in the playground for the bell, I spat nonchalantly on the ground.

The modern, two-storey school building, which was constructed of a dark red brick and had been erected only a dozen years before, seemed to me oppressive. The big sports hall and gymnasium at the school which had so impressed me when our class from junior school visited, now simply didn't register. And though I couldn't possibly have failed to notice the school's huge, well tended playing fields, even they made no ameliorating impression on my state of mind. This was obviously a school that took sport seriously, and sport, I already knew, was my lifeline. But on that first day, as I spat again on the unfriendly concrete ocean in front of the school, I thought I was going to drown.

Inside, Culverhouse was a warren of hostile corridors that all seemed to lead to the wrong room. It was a strange, bustling city, not an ocean. I now had to hurry from one classroom to another for different lessons. On the first day I got lost three times. I felt like I was in a foreign country – like a baby who fell asleep in her pram in the local park and woke up alone in the middle of the rush hour in Peking. Not Alice in Wonderland, but Alice in Nightmare Land.

When I caught a glimpse of Miss Meredith, the unfriendly deputy head, in her tweed skirt and pale, elegant blouse which had a neat bow at the neck, I didn't say hello. What was the point? So far as she was concerned, I was already tried and convicted.

If you're called the name, play the game, the saying goes. 'Miss, Miss, Miss,' I called out in my first class that first day, and then

65

asked a question, the same one the teacher had just answered. In the next classroom, and the next, I did the same. Pretending to the world that I felt very secure, I fell back on my old routine of playing up as much as I could. I was a pest. If I couldn't cope with school it would have to learn to cope with me.

7

Changes

I was now quite a well-built young lady for my age and needed to wear a bra. Mrs Smith didn't seem to notice this, although she quickly noticed even my slightest infraction of the rules. At school people did notice, and made the odd remark. I was beginning to get a bit self-conscious.

Auntie Rae had a word with Mrs Smith, who reluctantly agreed to part with some clothing vouchers. Auntie Rae and I set off for the shops to buy the bra. *En route* to Marks and Spencer's she somehow made me feel both that what was happening to my body was quite normal and that because of it, I was very special. My initial self-consciousness at this time was the only anguish I ever had over puberty.

As usual, Auntie Rae and I had a good time shopping, although, of course, we no longer walked along hand in hand. I was much too grown up. We bought a teen bra, a white cotton one, of which I was very proud.

I was now more than twelve and the oldest girl at the home. But just as I had when I first arrived, I shared a bedroom with other girls of all ages, including, whenever we had one, the baby-of-the-moment. Changing my clothes now became an intricate, irritating manoeuvre. The little ones were fascinated by the changes in my body, and they were young enough to stare whenever I stripped off. Like most adolescent girls, I felt modest. Either I queued for the toilet or bathroom in my pyjamas and held up the rest of the queue while I stayed there to change into my white school blouse and black skirt, or I grabbed my clothes and changed surreptitiously under the blankets.

What I longed for and sometimes daydreamed about was having a room of my own. The tiny staff bedroom well down the corridor was sometimes vacant for weeks at a time, even longer. I not only wanted, but needed a single bedroom, and this one was spare. By rights, I felt it should be mine. By experience, I knew Mrs Smith might feel otherwise, and that I must broach the subject delicately. I remember waiting politely in the lounge till she had a moment for me. When, at last, she did, her welcome was brusque, something in the order of, 'What is it now, Fatima?'

'I am getting to be,' I began hesitantly, 'a young lady.' Mrs Smith understood my meaning. 'I want the room that's going,' I blurted out before I could stop myself. 'I want to have my own room. I need it, Auntie Brenda. Please.'

'I'll have to think about who deserves the room most,' she said. 'And discuss it with Uncle Alan.'

My heart sank. 'But I need my privacy.'

'Don't we all,' she retorted. She promised she and Uncle Alan would decide in due course.

I hoped and hoped, but knew better than to expect much.

The Smiths took great pleasure in allocating the room to Sham, who was the eldest boy. To be fair, he was more than a year older than me, but I was convinced they were showing favouritism. If you were slightly cheeky to a thirty-hour lady or did something untoward at school, Sham told the Smiths. He was a sneak. Mrs Smith liked him because he gave her plenty of excuses to tell whoever it was off.

One evening, as I was about to go to bed, I noticed that on the end of our row of shoes – we placed our shoes for the next morning in a line in the hallway – was a new pair of pricey leather boots. I guessed they belonged to Sham and was incensed.

My only shoes were serviceable, brown leather ones. They were ugly and the very cheapest available, their only advantage being that although they looked sturdy, they soon wore out. I despised them. All of us children in the home were badly dressed and horrendously shod. But I should have been grateful for the leather shoes I called 'honky-clonks', because before I got them, even in winter, I only had plimsolls. These cost almost nothing and looked it. They were not at all fashionable the way trainers are today. They were an emblem of poverty, a dead give-away to anyone on the street that I was from the home. My toes got cold too and there was no support. At one point I had high-top basketball boots, with plastic discs at the ankle, which were slightly better. But the toes of those soon wore out. Then the horrible 'honky-clonks' were foisted upon me. I was never allowed to buy the sort of shoes I wanted. It was a sore point.

I knocked on the door of Sham's room to ask him how much the boots had cost.

'Thirteen quid.' He was smirking. 'Aren't they terrific?'

Thirteen pounds. I could hardly believe it. That was a fortune for shoes at the time. I went straight downstairs and asked to speak with Mr and Mrs Smith, who were busy watching television. Mrs Smith poked her head out to say that I could not talk to them then and that I was to go to bed.

'I'm fed up with the way I get treated around here,' I said. 'You always try deliberately to upset me. But you're terrible to all of us children. It is not fair. Something ought to be done about it. Where Alma is, things are entirely different. Better. Much better. So it's not just that this is a home. It's your fault, and Uncle Alan's.' The words came tumbling out.

I knew that the Smiths were allocated a clothing allowance for each child, and it seemed to me that we could not possibly be getting all the clothes we were entitled to. 'I'm going to report you to my social worker next time he calls in,' was my parting shot.

'Go to bed,' said Mrs Smith through clenched lips. 'Immediately.'

Needless to say, I got no joy on the clothing issue from either of them that night. And I did not get a new pair of shoes. I did inform my social worker who told me that the Smiths were kind people. And then, to my amazement, he went and told them I had complained.

After that my relationship with the Smiths deteriorated even further. There was nothing I would or could do to make them like me now. And just about anything I did made them flare up at me. Trying to be almost a mother to the younger ones, I would stand up for them – which Mrs Smith would have described as meddling. It was meddling, but I felt it was right and necessary.

Another bone of contention was the baby-of-the-moment. I was losing an awful lot of sleep looking after her when she cried during the night. Lifting her out of the cot and cradling her till she went back to sleep was the only way to stop her wailing. But she woke up all through the night. I was beginning to look haggard, and to feel tired all the time, and irritable, but the Smiths didn't want to know.

One night I banged on their bedroom door and demanded that they take care of the baby. When they shouted at me to go away, I kept pounding on the door until Mr Smith opened it. He glared at me and said in a tone of voice as icy as Antarctica, that I must not ever knock on their door again.

But there was another, more turbulent problem looming, one that was poles apart from my difficulty with the Smiths. It began when I was summoned peremptorily one Friday morning during the school holidays to the dining room because the woman who said she was my mother, had turned up. With her were three greasy-looking men. Aliya was there too, sitting primly next to her mother who had come to take her to London for the weekend. I wasn't at all glad to see any of them, but when I arrived, wearing the pink crimplene dress which had just been bought for me with clothing vouchers, one of the men smacked his lips and nodded at the others. I wasn't pleased either when Aliya's mother announced that for once I too was going to London for the weekend.

'I'm not going,' I said flatly.

The rest of the conversation went something like this: 'But I want both of my daughters at home.' Her tone was stagily dramatic. '*Both*.'

One of the men winked at his friend. The way those men were eyeing me up and winking was making me increasingly nervous.

'You can't make me go.'

Aliya's mother began to scream at me. 'You are my daughter. You must come.'

Cooling off on a hot summer's day in the back garden at Wormley Hill. Cory, in the background, is keeping an eye on us. I am the one with the hose.

Enjoying myself too much to mind that the coat was a hand-me-down, as was the tricycle.

These snapshots taken when I was nearly four are my only 'baby pictures'.

(CENTRE) Cory holding baby Julie. I am in the middle and Michael, the boy who was so fond of his red toy bus, is far left.

A school photograph of me, aged eleven.

(ABOVE) Victorious Thurrock Ladies Hockey Club with their umpire. Mum (back left) played centre forward and I (front right) played centre half.

(RIGHT) Mum bought me the leather jacket I had always wanted when I first came to stay with the Whitbreads.

(OPPOSITE BELOW) Auntie Rae with two boys from the children's home in 1972.

(ABOVE) Not even Virginia Wade, who won the Wimbledon title the day before, could have been more thrilled than I was to be Southern Counties intermediate champion. Crystal Palace, 1977.

(OPPOSITE) Mum, the boys and me, holding the Southern Counties trophy and the Victrix Ludorum, both of which I won on the same golden weekend in 1977.

(OVERLEAF) Winning the European Junior Championship, my first great victory, Poland, 1979. [*Tony Duffy, Allsport*]

(INSET) British athletes jumping for joy and TSB. I am in the centre.

California 1979.
(ABOVE) A harness-run on the sand. My young brothers help. Laguna Beach. [*Tony Duffy, Allsport*]

(OPPOSITE) The T-shirt says it all: 'Fatima's my name, Javelin's my game, Gold's my aim'.

(ABOVE) The trip to California wasn't all training runs. This is the photo I later sent to Steve.

Eight Nations Tournament, Peking 1980.
(OPPOSITE) My first trip to the Orient – China and Japan – to represent Britain. [*Tony Duffy, Allsport*

(ABOVE) In China do as the Chinese – the British team at the athletes' gala banquet, Eight Nations Tournament. [*Tony Duffy, Allsport*]

Moscow Olympics, 1980
(OPPOSITE) Heartbroken because I didn't even qualify for the final. Tessa didn't either.
[*Tony Duffy, Allsport*]

(OPPOSITE) Training near home, aged nineteen. [*Tony Duffy, Allsport*]

ABOVE) Coaching disabled children at Hornchurch track in Upminster, 1981. [*Tony Duffy, Allsport*]

Throwing for Britain, 1981.
[*Tony Duffy, Allsport*]

Releasing the javelin with a howl. Crystal Palace, 1981. [*Tony Duffy, Allsport*]

Cyprus, 1981. [*Tony Duffy, Allsport*]

(OPPOSITE) The Olympic shotput champion Udo Beyer of East Germany is a softie. European Championships, Athens, 1982. [*Tony Duffy, Allsport*]

(ABOVE) The American runner Valerie Brisco-Hooks who won gold at 200 and 400 metres in Los Angeles 1984. [*Ms Mamta Kapoor*]

(OPPOSITE) Donna Hartley, former Commonwealth 400 metres champion and a friend, spurs me to a 24.35-second 200 metres finish at the British training camp in Lanzarote.

The World Championships, Helsinki, Finland, 1983.
(ABOVE) The throw that so nearly won gold.

(OPPOSITE) I had thrown down the gauntlet.

(ABOVE) But on the last throw at the World Championships my gold turned to silver and I wept. Mum comforts me.

(OPPOSITE) Congratulating the victor, Tiina Lillak of Finland.

(OPPOSITE) Silver for me, gold for Tiina (centre), and bronze for Anna Verouli of Greece at the World Championships, 1983.

(ABOVE) Mum, Dad, my brothers and me in Lanzarote.

(RIGHT) Grandad and Nan, Jim and Maud Callender.

(ABOVE) Training at Crystal Palace, 1984. [D. Hooley, News of the World]

The Olympics, Los Angeles, 1984.
(OPPOSITE ABOVE) Congratulating Tessa on her Olympic victory. Tiina Lillak (left) won silver and won the bronze.

(OPPOSITE BELOW) Sharing our joy – Mum, me, Tessa and her coach.

(ABOVE) Proud Mum, at home, 1984.

European Championships, Stuttgart, 1986.
(OPPOSITE ABOVE) Concentrating. [*Sven Simon*]

(OPPOSITE BELOW) Seconds before the moment of release. [*Sven Simon*]

(OVERLEAF) I couldn't resist a victory wiggle when I threw 77.44 metres, setting a new world record. The West German thrower Beate Peters was pleased for me.

I shouted back. Perhaps the words 'fat old cow' escaped my lips.

'Come, girl,' one of the men said to me, in accented English. 'We must go now. Is late.'

'I'm not coming with you. I'm not.'

The men began to shout at Aliya's mother in the foreign language.

Hearing virtual mayhem coming from the dining room, Auntie Rae rushed in to see what the trouble was. She took one look at the three men and at Aliya's mother and knew immediately that if they took me away, it was not going to be for my own good. She said she wouldn't hear of it. But the men glowered and Aliya's mother insisted, implying that she had permission from Mrs Smith who was away for the weekend. At last, Auntie Rae, who was getting angrier and angrier, said in a tone of voice I had never heard her use before, that she had better have a little chat with Mrs Smith and she went to ring her at her weekend house.

Aliya, her mother, the three men and I waited uneasily. Edna, who did the cleaning, came in to do some dusting. While Edna wiped the table and the others jabbered amongst themselves in their language, I strained to hear Auntie Rae.

'Those men are up to no good,' she told Mrs Smith. 'But the woman says it's fine with you, for Fatima to go to London.' Mrs Smith said there was always trouble where Fatima was concerned. At last Auntie Rae exploded: 'In no circumstances will I let Fatima go,' she said.

When she hung up the receiver, Auntie Rae told Aliya's mother that she would not permit me to go. For the moment, that was the end of that. But I was still shaking when I heard the front door slam behind them. I did not know what exactly I was frightened of, but Auntie Rae and Edna thought they knew. Years later Auntie Rae told me I would have been lucky had it ended there. 'I suspected those men wanted to put you on the game.' If they did have prostitution in mind, my supposed mother didn't notice.

Following this incident I asked Mrs Smith to arrange another meeting with my social worker. Nothing happened. I asked her again and again, and she always said that she had forwarded my request. But it was not until some months later, when we were approaching the school summer holidays, that the social worker visited me. Tall, dark, and earnest, Mr Walker was thirty or thereabouts, a few years younger than the Smiths and a completely different kettle of fish.

As Edna put it, Mrs Smith tried to give an upstairs-downstairs impression to everyone including the staff, who would remind her that they were not her personal servants, but were, as she was, hired by the council to look after the children. Whereas Mr Walker, who was quite well-spoken, had the nervous air of a naive and very young public school boy who has stumbled into a dockers' brawl. For all I know he may have been a coal-miner's son, but there was something of the young Robert Redford in his looks and something about his gentle, reasonable manner and his suit and tie, that made one feel he had grown up in another world, one in which family members were middle-class and always very well-meaning. He probably wanted to save the world, a perfectly proper aim for a social worker, I think. But he went by the book too much; he didn't use his instinct or his head. I thought that, as a social engineer, he was cack-handed.

When finally he paid me a visit, Bob Walker immediately made sympathetic noises and took me for a walk in the park. But when I told him of all my problems, he said I must be exaggerating because he had always found Mrs Smith to be a pleasant, sympathetic and interested matron.

'But she's a con artist. She puts on a show when you arrive. Don't you see?'

Now he was certain that I was exaggerating, perhaps having a bit of teenage rebellion.

'Talk to the day ladies. They will confirm my stories.'

And they did. Forthright Auntie Rae and even more forthright Edna had plenty of bitter stories of their own to tell. But the social worker just didn't want to know. To put off Auntie Rae, he warned her that if he had a serious chat with her, he would have to tell Mrs Smith. When Auntie Rae said, 'I don't mind if you tell her,' he still kept his distance.

I couldn't understand his reasoning at all then, but I do now. If he had admitted to himself that the Smiths were a problem, he would have had terrible trouble. First he would have had to say to his superiors that he and they had made a big mistake in employing the Smiths. Then he would have had to prove it. Imagine the attendant aggro and legal snarls, and the costs – both in time and that scarce commodity, DHSS money. And then, after all that, he would have had to find a new matron or resettle all the children that were fostered there. No one can entirely blame him for not being ready or able to take on the issue of the Smiths, and for telling himself that there was no issue, just a teenager's exaggeration. I shudder to think how often and to how many children this sort of thing may have happened. Isn't there something someone, anyone, can do?

I do blame Bob Walker for his next ploy. What he did – again probably not realising what he was doing – was to use my so-called exaggerations about the Smiths against me. I couldn't get on with the Smiths, he felt, because what I really wanted was my mother. And he had come prepared with a solution to that. He had a surprise for me. Dear God, it was a whopper. Aliya's mother – the woman who had brought along the very men about whom I had been consulting Mr Walker – wanted to make a big effort to bring the family together at last.

As we trudged through the park, Mr Walker grew hoarse trying to convince me that the woman loved me and had always loved me, but not until now had she been able to look after me properly. Indeed not. When I had gone along with Aliya for the day, the woman was either 'looking after' her man or looking after Aliya and herself. I was not a top priority except when she needed someone to plead with the milkman not to stop deliveries because of the unpaid bill.

But now, according to Mr Walker, she wanted to have me at home with her. *Because she loved me!* He was immensely pleased, he said. I could tell from the sincere crack in his voice and his furrowed brow that he meant it.

Kicking a stone out of my path, I said something rude. You couldn't really excuse a social worker for being innocent as a new born babe. It was his job to be knowing.

The plan was that I would go to stay with Aliya's mother and Aliya in London for a while to try it out. It might lead, Mr Walker said enthusiastically, to a visit of months or even forever. I could not believe that he could be so naive as to swallow that line after all these years.

'I'm not going anywhere near her,' I said defiantly.

If I was so unhappy at the Smiths', he argued, I ought to look on this as a promising development. It was desirable, he explained, again puckering his brow, that every effort be made to bring a family together. Because the woman who they said was my mother had requested it, he was bound to do it.

My heart sank. I was between the devil and the deep blue sea. And I couldn't make him understand. It looked as though my best hope was to drown. But I'm a fighter. 'I'm a ward of the court,' I said. 'I don't have to go.'

But I did.

On a hazy, humid morning early in the summer holidays when I would much rather have been arguing with Uncle Alan, Aliya and I caught a Green Line bus to London. Then we changed buses and finally got off not far from the front door.

The flat was in an unlovely block, amid other ugly blocks, edging the busy road. To me they all looked equally uninviting, but Aliya knew which was the one. We trudged up to the top floor. At each landing we saw obscene words scrawled on the walls in big letters and inhaled the stench of urine. At first, I thought the people who lived in these flats did not have toilets.

Inside the flat, the woman and her son were waiting. Nearly a man now at fifteen or sixteen, Adem had hefty shoulders and an air of Mediterranean macho. But the anger that had always been lurking just beneath the surface was still there. Just as he had done when we were children, Adem scowled at me. I scowled back.

As soon as we got inside the front door, Aliya was hugged and kissed by her mother and welcomed by him. The three of them began to chatter in their language, which they knew I didn't understand. Ignored, I slumped against the wall of the hallway, crammed between Adem and a little table they had there near the door.

But I was not ignored for long. The woman soon set me to cleaning the balding lino on the kitchen floor. Although the kitchen, which was in a state, was minuscule, the lino was so encrusted with dirt that I thought it would take a week of hard scrubbing. And, she said, as soon as I had finished the floor, I was to start immediately on the greasy, chipped cooker which was missing most of its knobs and looked as though it had last been cleaned before detergent was invented.

Adem went to his room to read, and the woman and Aliya went out to do some shopping. She told me with hand signals that I must not run away. How could I? Aliya had been our navigator. I had no money and little idea of what bus to take or where to take it.

Like Cinderella, I turned my attention to the scrubbing. I found some rags and a filthy sponge to scrub with, but the only bucket I could see was full up with something thick and creamy which looked less like whipped cream than pea soup, although it was dead white. I dared not tip it out without permission.

When I asked Adem what I should do, he laughed and said that he would show me at tea what to do with home-made yoghurt. He found me another bucket, but suggested with a smile that I let the cleaning wait a moment. He had something more interesting to show me now. He was being very genial, especially for him. Maybe the years had changed him, but I was concerned that Aliya and her mother would return and find the housework undone. Not to worry, Adem said, I had plenty of time to do the cleaning. When they went out, they always stayed away for hours.

As I followed him into the recesses of the flat, however, I did feel just a bit nervous. He led me into his mother's tiny bedroom, which was scarcely big enough for the double bed. The bedhead was pushed against the wall, leaving barely enough room to walk around the bed, which had a multi-coloured quilt thrown over it. The room was tidy, almost clean – she evidently took more care of her room than the rest of the flat. It was a room with an urban view. The flat was high up, perhaps on the sixth floor. When

Adem showed me out on to the tiny balcony, I could see the car-park in the forecourt with Cortinas and Minis and even a taxi parked in there. Adem told me to wait there, and he rushed out and returned with a balloon full of water. We dropped the balloon and laughed.

I was beginning to like him. With a bright smile, he announced he had something else to show me. To my astonishment, it was a dirty magazine. The boys at school had magazines like that but I had never paid them any attention. When Adem began flicking through the pages, urging me to look, I took a step back towards the door. But he stepped quickly in front of me, pulling my hand from the brass doorknob and pushing me on to the bed. Holding me under him, he tried to make me look at the pictures of naked men and women in the magazine.

'This is beyond a joke,' I said, hoping I sounded fierce rather than frightened and struggling to get up. Let me go, Adem.' I spat on the magazine, refusing to look at it.

We fought viciously. All that was going through my mind was, I'll kill him first. Or he'll kill me. I think he got the message that it wasn't by any means foreplay. Suddenly he pushed me over, grabbed the magazine and rushed out of the room, locking the door behind him.

I banged and banged on the door and tried to pull it open. I had won, but at the same time I had lost. I felt so defeated because I was beginning to realise I couldn't win here. Adem hadn't got what he wanted, but when the woman got back and the floor was in the same dire state as when she went out, and I was in her room. It didn't bear thinking about. I lay on her bed seething with hopelessness and anger.

Shortly before the woman and Aliya returned, Adem unlocked the door.

'Don't you dare say anything,' he said, or words to that effect. 'I was just letting you have a look. I wouldn't have really done anything.'

I wondered. But I didn't have time to be upset or even angry. I rushed to get started on the kitchen. Aliya and the woman would soon be back. It was too late to get very much done. On her return, the woman beat me with the flat of her hand for not having finished the cleaning. I didn't dare tell her why. Anyway, I couldn't. We could only communicate in the most rudimentary fashion and then only with Adem's help. He would do a semi-translation, and I knew he wouldn't translate any complaints I made against him.

I'm not sure she would have cared anyway. And I doubt that she would ever have told him to back off. First of all, he was menacing – perhaps, like me, she was a bit afraid of him. He has since been in trouble with the police. When I bumped into his sister Emmie a few years ago, she told me he was in prison for grievous bodily harm. And secondly, Adem helped his mother make ends meet. When one morning he came in with a bottle of milk he had stolen from the milk float whilst the milkman was delivering to the other flats in the building, the woman patted him on the back. Thirdly, Adem was her mouthpiece. She needed him to translate her orders to me for the housework. The woman would wave a forefinger in my face and say something I only half understood.

'Go on, do it,' Adem would say. 'Clean out the fridge.' Or 'Gather up the washing. Now!'

What I did understand when she said it, and what she took pride in saying in a dozen little ways was, 'I don't love you.' I can only think she brought me out of the home because she needed a skivvy, someone to do the cleaning and to babysit for Aliya when she was otherwise occupied.

The woman had a man staying with her, a Turkish Cypriot, who came and went. He had a thick black moustache, and stubble, and he stank of booze. Stocky with a bit of a paunch, he was always coming out of the bedroom, usually with no shirt on, sometimes clad only in his underpants. He didn't ever seem to bother to comb his greasy dark hair.

During the past year on the two other occasions I had come with Aliya for the day, the man was there. Occasionally in the afternoon, he and she would disappear into the bedroom, as they did in the evening. I don't think he worked because when he was out he must have been drinking. He would come in reeking of alcohol and sit in the big armchair in the corner of the lounge, scratching at his bare, hairy chest, watching telly with us, and making silly comments about the huge photograph of the woman which was hanging on the wall above the shabby settee, where I slept at night. The photograph was a head and shoulders shot of her smiling and looking younger and much thinner. She wore a rhinestone tiara. In the photo, she wasn't bad looking. The man would make his comments in their language, but the gist of it was that he wished he had known her then. I don't think the man contributed much money to the household. Certainly not enough. The woman was always pulling pound notes out of her bra, counting them, and finding she didn't quite have enough.

It may have been the Easter holiday because the three of us, Adem, Aliya and I caught a bus to the local fun fair. I couldn't believe that Cinderella was being allowed to go to the fair. But we had to be home by the stroke of ten o'clock, not midnight. I rarely went anywhere interesting, and had only just got the courage to go out on errands. When I went outside I was confused because there were so many blocks of flats in the street and they all looked the same to me. I was scared for a moment that I was lost, and certain that if I went further afield I would be. To my amazement, when I got back and I mentioned this, the woman made Adem write down the address of the flat on a piece of paper for me. She told me to make certain that whenever I went out, I had the address in my pocket.

The fun fair was magic, although Aliya and I lost sight of Adem almost immediately. He was supposed to be looking after us – and he was the one who knew the way home, but almost as soon as we got there, he went off with some girl he had begun chatting up.

I was entranced by the fun fair. I liked the animated music, and the happy screeches of the children and even the adults on the rides. Aliya and I went on one of them that jiggled us about frantically and we screamed too. There were mostly young couples at the fair, walking hand in hand, although there were also plenty of dads holding on to their young children's hands. I liked the smell of the popcorn, but Aliya and I didn't have enough money left between us to buy any. What little we had, we spent on throwing hoops to win a fish. My throw wasn't good enough to win us one. At least when you throw a javelin, it doesn't have to land in a precise spot.

The time went quickly. Adem had disappeared with our return bus money, and when it became clear that he wasn't looking for us, being older, I took charge. I led Aliya into the main street, hailed a taxi cab and gave him the piece of paper with the address written on it. When he arrived the taxi driver was afraid we would run off without paying, so Aliya waited in the taxi while I hurried up to the flat to get the fare from her mother.

When Aliya's mother opened the door and saw that Aliya was not with me, she was outraged and dragged me in. Then she threw me on to the floor and began bashing me up. She was unable to understand my explanation, and unwilling even to try. 'Taxi,' I said. 'Aliya downstairs, in taxi.' As I pointed desperately towards the street, the woman picked up the little hall table and smashed it across my back, again and again, until mercifully the table broke. Whatever English she possessed had deserted her, she was in such a terrible rage.

She was jabbering at me in Cypriot, and I at her in English. I was frightened, and becoming hysterical myself, when she ran into the kitchen and came out with a bread knife. At this point the din was such that the man in her bed woke up, and came running out of the bedroom dressed only in his grey-white underpants.'*Polizia, polizia*,' he said to her, grabbing the knife. 'Neighbours will report.' There were pillow marks on his face, and his bushy hair was messier than ever. As usual he stank of alcohol, but I was glad to see him.

At last I was able to get a word in: 'Aliya is in the taxi waiting.' I ran to the door and pointed out the taxi's headlamps in the street. The man understood. He told her, and thankfully she did not hit me when he went to the bedroom to get some pound notes, which he put in my hand. I ran down the stairs and paid the fare. The taxi driver had kept the meter going. When Aliya and I got back to the flat, I made her walk in ahead of me, but her mother and the man had disappeared into the bedroom.

Aliya and I were dog-tired. It was nearly eleven at night. She went to her bedroom in the front of the flat to sleep, and I went to the lounge. As I pulled the blanket over me on my settee bed, my mind was racing. Life was becoming a waking nightmare. Just before I fell asleep, I heard the front door open and Adem sneak into his room with a girlfriend. They were whispering and giggling.

Much later something woke me with a start. It was the door of the lounge opening. I was too frightened to ask who it was. I thought perhaps I was dreaming, since when I opened my mouth nothing came out. In the dark I could sense rather than see someone walking towards the couch where I was lying. Then I could smell the booze on him as he walked into the armchair and swore.

I was panic-stricken, literally frozen with terror, utterly unable to move, hoping he was just looking for something he had left in the lounge. He found it all right. It was me. When he lay on the couch alongside me. I kept very still, pretending to be asleep. He moved closer. Slowly, as though I was moving in my sleep, I inched away, into the back of the settee, creating a sliver of space between us. I hoped he would get the message and go away. Instead he started to touch me. He stank of alcohol and sweat. I pushed him away with my feet. He began to pull at my pyjamas but was too drunk to get them off.

I was terrified and could not believe this was happening. I pulled away. He tried to thrust upon me from behind. I couldn't move. I was in a state of panic, but at least I was able to scream. 'No! no!,' I shouted. 'Help! Someone help me!'

He tried to muffle my screams by pushing my head into the couch. With sudden strength, he pulled off my pyjamas and thrust into me. It hurt. I kept shouting and pulling away from him. I was fighting in earnest now, screaming at every possible moment, desperately hoping that one of the others would decide to come to my rescue. He clung to me tightly, panting.

Eventually the woman came running into the front room. When she switched on the light, she saw he was stark naked and in bed with me. She glared at both of us, as though we were in collusion. Then Adem rushed in, followed by Aliya. The woman was screaming in Cypriot and the only word I could pick out was *'Polizia'*. Two hours before, he had threatened her with the police, now she was threatening him. That got him out of the room and back into her bedroom.

They all went back to bed with hardly a word to me. I was sobbing, but I got out of the makeshift bed to lock the door behind them. It wouldn't lock. It was cold and I got back under the covers, a total wreck, praying for morning to come quickly.

As I lay there in the dark, wishing I could sleep, but listening anxiously to the night noises, thinking each one must be him, I wondered how the social worker could possibly have imagined that this was the family I should live in. The woman had shown me no love since I had arrived. She had more concern for the state of her kitchen floor. And now, after her lover had raped me, no doubt she blamed me.

I heard the toilet flush, and then the doorknob being turned. I sat up with a start. I could not believe it was happening again. I hurriedly got out of the bed and hid behind the armchair. He was trying to find me again, but the woman, guessing he would make a detour, called out to him. He left to go back to her.

I knew he could come again later in the night when I had fallen asleep, and I knew I couldn't face even the thought of it happening again. Timidly I knocked on Adem's door, and pleaded with him to let me sleep there on the floor. Adem was sure the man wouldn't try it yet again, and said no. Besides, his girlfriend was still there. I went back to the lounge but I knew I didn't dare go to sleep. Leaving the light on, I sat hunched under the blanket, alone and scared.

Suddenly, I heard the door of the woman's bedroom open again. Perhaps it was her, not him. Surely Adem was right, he wouldn't dare try his luck again. I switched the light out and hid once more behind the armchair. I could hear my heart pounding. I hoped he couldn't. But, I told myself, I was a fool, scaring myself for nothing, I had to calm down – it couldn't be him. But it was.

I could not stand the pressure of this any longer. I had to get out of that room or I would go mad. As he crept in, befuddled by the dark and the drink, I ran towards the doorway, which I could just make out in the moonlight. I ran into him as I tried to get out of the room. He stumbled as I brushed past, trying to gather himself and grab me at the same time. But it was too late, I was out of the room and pounding on Adem's door, screaming and sobbing, shouting, a mass of turbulent emotions.

Suddenly, they were all in the corridor again, the woman screaming at the man and at me. 'If you tell anyone this,' she said, 'I kill you.' I went into Adem's room and stood huddled with my back against the cold wall. The girl in his bed said nothing. When Adem had quieted his mother, he came back into the bedroom, carrying my blanket, and locked the door. He told me I could sleep in his room on the floor.

Later, when his girlfriend left, he went into the lounge to sleep and left me his bed. I locked the door and lay down exhausted in the rumpled bed. But I soon fell asleep. I dreamt the nightmare that had followed me from childhood. The man in the cape was ringing the bell with a toilet chain, ringing and ringing. The noise of the bell clanging was thunderous, even though the man had stopped pulling the chain and was now chasing me. I woke with a start. I hadn't wet Adem's bed, but I knew I was beyond sleep.

Morning took what seemed like two centuries to arrive. Bedraggled physically and emotionally, I knew I had to leave that flat. I had no money, and was uncertain as to which bus to take. I only knew I was going. As soon as he was up, I pleaded with Adem to help me to get back to the children's home. He told me this was my home, the place where I belonged.

'No, no, no, no,' I said, almost in a whisper, too exhausted to shout. 'I can't stay here.' He could hear the rock hard determination in my quiet voice. He knew I didn't know the way or have the fare, but Adem finally realised that I was going to leave whatever. Then he offered to give me the bus fare if I kept quiet about what had happened.

I would have agreed to any suggestion to get away from that flat. I knew I had to get away, I had to get back to the home, which at that moment seemed like a haven.

8

Troubled

The house was empty when I arrived. Because there was no pounding of buses and heavy lorries past the windows like there was in London, the house seemed eerily quiet. Inside my head, though, there was uproar. When I thought about what had happened – what the man had done to me which could not be undone, and that terrible word *rape*; when I thought about Aliya's mother threatening to kill me – and I could not seem to stop thinking about it – I began to tremble, my fingers twitching as though they were in the midst of a terrifying nightmare.

After unpacking from a carrier bag the few things I had taken with me – a jumper, underwear, my comb which was missing more than a few teeth, a hair brush, a toothbrush – I went downstairs into the kitchen to make myself a hot drink. It didn't matter to me one bit that we were forbidden to enter the kitchen except when told, and I didn't give a toss that Mrs Smith might at any moment come striding in. I badly needed the warmth and comfort of a steaming cup of tea. And I needed and wanted to go to see Auntie Rae, to tell her what had happened, to get comfort from her. But I felt so ashamed.

As I put the teabag into a chipped mug and waited for the kettle to boil, my eyes welled with sudden tears, my heart beat in angry despair. Yet I felt that I was both me and a fly on the wall watching me. I was watching myself getting out the tea things, pulling out the kitchen chair, brushing the few crumbs off the table. It was an eerie, uncomfortable feeling, as though I were coming apart into two separate bits. The hot tea warmed my shaking fingers, but it could not warm the chill I felt inside. I wanted to knock on Auntie

83

Rae's door. I wanted to see her, and talk to her, but equally I knew I could not.

It seemed to take hours to drink the tea, and then I watched myself washing up the mug and carefully drying it so that Mrs Smith would not know that I had broken yet another of her silly rules. I stared at myself walking out of the kitchen and out of the back door, and then I realised that I was walking towards the children's home where my friend Alma lived. Because she was a year younger than me and had absolutely no idea that such terrible things happened, with Alma I could pretend that they didn't.

Turning the corner, I marvelled at the stillness of everything. In comparison with London, this part of Essex seemed to be a rustic Arcadia.

At Alma's, the person that rang the bell was greeted with an enthusiastic hello, Alma ecstatic to see me back so soon. Neither she nor any of the other children noticed the sad, weepy person that was staring down from the wall. We went in a noisy, good-natured, straggly parade to the park and threw a ball around.

Returning to the home, my depression surfaced again, and I opened the door willing myself to veil my feelings sufficiently to show absolutely nothing to Mrs Smith. But instead Auntie Rae was there, wiping the kitchen table. She had been on all weekend, out on an errand that morning when I had first come back. If only I had known.

'Something terrible has happened, Aunt,' I blurted out. 'But I can't tell.' Sobs wracked my body; I thought I was going to burst with grief.

Auntie Rae put her arms around me. 'What is it?' I was shaking, the tears streaming down my cheeks. 'Lovie, what's the matter?'

'Aliya's mother said she would kill me if I told anyone.'

'I'm not anyone. You sit down, Fats, and tell me everything. You will feel better, love, when you do.'

I was afraid to tell her, but I was also afraid of not telling because I so needed her to know. Perching on the edge of the kitchen table, I said in a solemn but shaky voice, 'I'll tell you only if you promise not to tell anyone.'

'I won't be able to keep it a secret if it's important, love.'

I began to cry softly, and she put her arms back around me. Despite my tears, my sobs of pain, the whole awful story began to pour out. Even after I had finished telling it, I continued to cry on Auntie Rae's shoulder. Even when she said, 'I can't keep that secret. That's got to be reported,' I felt better. Auntie Rae helped me to tidy myself up and put me to bed. Later she told Mrs Smith and when nothing seemed to come of it, I felt safe.

Mrs Smith, whose duty it was, promised she would report the incident to head office. When Auntie Rae inquired the next day or the day after that, she said she had rung them, that the authorities had sent someone over to the flat in London but that the man was not there so that nothing could be done. There was no official inquiry, and when Margaret Whitbread was shown my case history some months later, there was no mention at all of sexual abuse.

Auntie Rae and I didn't talk about it either. What was there to say. It was not my fault, Auntie Rae had told me. There was no reason to feel dirty or ashamed. But as the weeks passed, the glum person on the wall looking down at me came more and more to the fore. The terrible time I had endured in London kept coming back to me. Even in the midst of playing ball or chatting with Alma and Wendy and my other friends, I would suddenly for no apparent reason drop into a state of deep gloom. This would alternate with feelings of rage.

I started to smoke. My arguments with Mrs Smith and her husband became increasingly bitter. Most mornings turned into squalls of emotion and then storms in which the least of what she said was that I was a troublemaker. I will never ever forget my shock and feeling of utter hopelessness, which quickly turned to anger, that terrible morning when she told me for the first time, 'It's obvious that no family will ever want *you*.' It wasn't the last time she said it either.

But I have to admit, I gave as good as I got, and by the time I got to school I was in no mood to be told anything by anyone. And certainly not to be asked some stupid question about Shakespeare or the capital of the Sudan. Not surprisingly I was always in trouble at school. I was lippy to the teachers. At that school,

85

they were used to it. They were ratty back to me, and I accepted it. I had to, didn't I? And it was their right. But I wouldn't take anything from the other pupils no matter how big they were. Anyone who was snotty with me, or even offhanded, had trouble on his hands.

There was a brawny lad who was a brutal, verbal bully. He was big-fisted and in the leather jacket set, but it was his loud mouth that bloodied. He called me a bastard and made certain everyone knew he meant it literally. He knew I lived in a children's home and what social liabilities that was likely to entail. He made certain everyone in the school knew, humiliating me relentlessly.

He towered over me, but at the first opportunity in the playground I stood up to him and, nervous though I was, I snarled, 'You were cheeky to me in maths and now you are going to get what I said you would get.'

He pushed me away.

'I said now you're gonna get what I promised you.'

'I don't fight girls,' he said. He looked at me like I was nothing. 'Fuck off.'

Instead, I let rip. I had to jump up to hit him, he was that much taller than I. He hit back, but he was trying not to fight because I was a girl. That was even more infuriating. He could get away with denigrating me in the classroom and now by not fighting he would humiliate me again. I hit and hit and hit him. A teacher had to pull us apart.

Only on the hockey field could I turn my frustration and aggression into something worthy of applause. There was only one of me, but that one was all over the field, wielding a hockey stick with a vengeance. Stay out of my way was the message. With netball, it was much the same story. It may have been a girls' game, but I was anything but a ladylike player.

On the court there was no gloomy me; no person watching from the sidelines or like a fly on the wall; I felt no sense of being split. There was only the one person, but that one had the strength and speed of seven. Little did I realise that sport was going to be my passport to the future, because even though I sensed that sport was now the only thing that was keeping me from drowning in despair, I didn't think about it much. To be absolutely honest, my life didn't really seem to be worth saving.

In fact, I was worried because for the first time, I was having trouble with PE lessons, that is, with country dancing, if you can call it PE. Not that I had any problems with dancing *per se* — but what we did at the disco on a Wednesday night was a far cry from country dancing. We wiggled and twisted and shook it up and down. Country dancing was all prim and pre-set, with movements just so; no life in it; no fun. I agreed wholeheartedly with Peter Townsend of the Who who prescribed rock and roll, where the music inspired you to dance your troubles away.

The teacher was the same stern, be-bunned deputy head, Miss Meredith, who had soured my impression of my secondary school when I came with my junior school class to look it over. Some years later, this same Miss Meredith, who mum tells me was a good teacher and had a lot to put up with in me, explained that my moods were a trial to her. Either I was feeling high, or terribly, terribly low — no in between for me. That I believe, but I have to say too that country dancing was, in my opinion, such a stupid bore that I did my best to avoid it. One out of three lessons would find me smoking in the girls' loos. And when I did turn up, I did my very best to disrupt the class, by making awkward remarks and dancing the wrong steps. If it was fast, I would move slowly; if it was a slow step, I would be lively. She got fed up. She would have had to be more than human not to.

When she was showing us some new dance, I will never forget, I began to do it in slow motion, and Miss Meredith, having grown pale with frustration at my behaviour, shouted, 'Move faster!'

Of course, I didn't.

'Move,' she said in an uncharacteristically fierce tone, 'move, move!' She swatted my legs with her open palm, hard.

I moved all right.

'Move, move!' Her words were in time to the music, 'Move!' She slapped my legs again.

I moved, and properly too.

'No more nonsense,' she said. She slapped again. 'Keep moving. It is time you condescended to join our class.'

87

In her heart of hearts, she must, like most of the other teachers whom I was giving a hard time, have wished I hadn't condescended even to come to class. The authorities were eventually alerted that something in my behaviour was deeply wrong. I was deemed intolerable, and a summit meeting was convened to decide what could be done about me. The school was on the verge of expelling me.

Mrs Smith didn't throw any official light on the reason for my troubled and troubling state perhaps because she wanted me out of her house. That would have meant moving me back to London, since it was a London council that still had charge of me. I was terrified of going to London, not just because of what had happened to me there, but because I knew that that was where lone girls got trapped by drugs and prostitution and poverty. It was the last place I wanted to go. Not that I was even consulted.

My fate was to be determined by the summit conference in which I did not even take part. Miss Toomey of the Finsbury district social services came from head office, accompanied by Bob Walker. As a pair they were utterly contrasting. She was a mousey, middle-aged, well-intentioned spinster whom it was easy to underestimate. She looked as though only saccharine ran in her veins, but she had the experience and the nous to suss out a problem quickly, and when the situation called for it, she had a surprisingly sharp tongue. That day the situation would call for it.

Bob Walker and his heart-breaking caution, I have already described. But together Toomey and Walker made a fairly formidable pair. That day when they sat down with a teacher I didn't know very well from my school and Mrs Smith, I was fortunate that they were batting for my side.

Before the summit Miss Toomey had a little chat with Auntie Rae, who was not invited to the meeting but who did after all know me the best. The conversation went something like this:

'But what's the matter with Fatima? Why can't the Smiths get on with the girl?' Miss Toomey asked.

'Because Fatima believes in justice and fair play.'

Miss Toomey did a double take. 'But at school she's a troublemaker too.'

'By the time she leaves here in the morning, the child is so

88

wound up, it's only her good nature that keeps her from setting the place on fire. You would be too, Miss Toomey, if you had Mrs Smith snarling at you, not to mention him, Mr Smith, on at you too.'

Auntie Rae was shooed out as the others arrived, and the meeting began, with the social workers, Toomey and Walker, arguing that I should stay at the home, largely on the grounds that I had been there a long time and had friends in the neighbourhood. It was a sort of 'better the devil you know' argument, based on the social worker's theory that what I seemed to need at the time was something to hang on to, stability – plus what Bob Walker thought of as Mrs Smith's benevolent influence and what Miss Toomey knew to be the lack of a suitable place for me in London.

Evidently, the school counsellor sided with the social workers, because after delicate negotiations this summit meeting decided I could stay on at the Smiths' – provided I went to see a child psychologist. Even the idea of it embarrassed me. But with the spectre of London looming and the glum, weepy person on the wall getting gloomier and ever more in attendance, I agreed to try it once. I had no choice.

With my fingers in my mouth and an ostentatiously cheerful Auntie Rae at my side, I boarded the Green Line bus for the journey to Grays. After what seemed like hours, but was in reality only about twenty minutes, we arrived. I was tense and slightly nauseous, Auntie Rae exhausted from all that joviality.

'Let's just go home,' I said when we got to the grimy, red brick building which housed the council's special medical services. The sky darkened. It was going to rain. 'I don't want to see any child psychologist.' I lowered my voice. 'I'm not crazy.'

'You're not in the least bit crazy.' Auntie Rae's tone was reassuring. 'But you do need help. Come along, Fats. We must do what we must do.'

As we procrastinated in the rain, a plump septuagenarian on slender, mismatched crutches brushed past into the building. 'He's a little old, isn't he?' I said. 'Aren't we supposed to be seeing a *child* psychologist?'

'They take the lame of all sorts here, Fats. Likely he has come to see one of the other doctors or for a new pair of crutches,' answered Auntie.

Slightly relieved that the passers-by could not know for certain why I was here, I followed the man on crutches inside to a perfectly ordinary waiting room, which was intentionally bland but much in need of paint, and I slumped into an uncomfortable little chair. But I was too restless to sit still for long and began to suck on my fingers again and to prowl about, feeling hostile and extremely embarrassed. I knew I wasn't crazy, just angry and confused – and with good reason. I didn't want a stranger messing about with my head.

Dr Dano motioned us into her office, where Auntie Rae with her coat in her lap and I, holding on to my jacket as if it were a life preserver, sat stiffly on the hard little chairs opposite the doctor's ugly but imposing desk. On the desk was an odd little contraption, a pole with a chain attached to it and a small ball suspended from the chain, which vaguely reminded me of the toilet chain in my recurring nightmare.

To break the ice, Dr Dano, a woman of sixty and quite unlike anyone I had ever met, flashed a gentle smile and quietly muttered some pleasantry in the order of, 'I am pleased to meet you.'

My hands began to shake. Another foreign accent. She was from Eastern Europe, I think, a short angular woman with glasses and lank, iron grey hair pulled back into a taut bun. She had on a tweed skirt, with the matching jacket slung over the back of her chair. She was an Eastern European blue stocking, someone utterly foreign to me. I didn't want to talk to her. So I didn't.

But the doctor was resourceful. Pointing to the ball on the chain on her desk, she asked me to hit it hard. 'Actions are plainer than words,' she said, 'aren't they?'

I swatted the ball. It spun on its chain just a bit.

'You can do much better than that, can't you, Fatima? Try now to think of someone you dislike, and then strike the ball again.'

Thinking of Mr and Mrs Smith, I hit the ball so hard that it pulled the chain nearly to breaking point.

The doctor was impressed. 'You must really hate the person or people about whom you were thinking.'

I nodded.

She seemed to feel that we had accomplished something, and said we would talk more at my next appointment. I think I went in three-week intervals.

'This is a waste of time,' I told Auntie Rae on the bus back to the home. 'I can't talk to that woman.'

'Do try, love.' Auntie Rae patted my hand. Out of the window there were grey skies. 'It may help, and unless your behaviour improves, I think the Smiths will get their way and you will be moved from the home to London.'

London was my worst thought. It meant I would have nowhere and no one. Tears welled in my eyes again. But I held them back because I certainly didn't want strangers staring at me on the Green Line bus.

'Look on the bright side,' Auntie Rae said. 'Life is about to get better. This woman doctor is here to help you do it faster, that's all.'

'It's a waste of time seeing her. I could be out at Blackshots doing some training,' I said morosely.

'Even without training you're the best athlete in the school, ain't you? No one can take that away from you.'

I smiled a little.

'I knew you would win the swimming gala at the school. You're the one who didn't want to go. What's it like this new sport, the javelin, isn't it?'

As I began to tell her everything I knew about the javelin, which was not much, and everything I knew about the javelin teacher, even less – but that didn't stop me talking – my spirits rose and rose.

Auntie Rae was a brilliant psychologist.

'Seems to me, Fats,' she said, certainly not referring to the weather, 'there is sunlight on the horizon.'

9

The Turning Point

It had been such a grating struggle just getting to be thirteen. I was beginning to think I had been born on a morning when God was having a lie-in. Was I going to spend the rest of my wretched life being horribly messed about? Would I always alternately seethe with rage or feel hopelessly, drearily bleak?

Even my lifeline – school sport – was keeping me only barely afloat. Sport, at which I excelled almost without even trying, made me feel I was somebody. And the aggression-releasing cut and thrust of netball, the bounding and the screams on court kept my feverish emotional temperature just below danger point. But with one thing and another – the aggro at school, the Smiths, the miserable encounters in London – I sometimes felt I was drowning in the ugly, stormy ocean that was my life.

Aliya's mother's only interest in me, and it still hurt, seemed to be as a scivvy. Nor had she protected me from her son's or her lover's unwelcome sexual advances. What happened to me in her flat, that horrible experience, was something I would never entirely get over. Doubt that I could hold on until I was rescued, doubt that I ever would be rescued brimmed ever more frequently. Nothing interested me.

I remember feeling on the day of a stupid netball match that our school was playing against stupid St Chad's School, that I was getting to the end of my tether. But if I could just get this bloody match over with, with some blessing – for the team, God, not me – then I would quietly lie down and wait for the rest of my wretched life to be over.

About half an hour later I met Mrs Whitbread, the no-nonsense umpire with a booming temper who so utterly changed my life. She was, I now realise, the spitting image of me, except for her colouring – the wan complexion which was typically English, as were her blue eyes and cropped, mousey hair. Hefty for her five-foot four-inch frame, chubby but with muscle under the skin, she was a PE teacher at St Chad's, who were our main rivals for the league title; yet we girls from our school were meekly supposed to accept that she was impartial when it came to umpiring this match.

Our own teacher, who lacked the one thing really necessary in a netball umpire, a loud, carrying voice, had let St Chad's do as they liked during the first half of the match. But when it was Mrs Whitbread's turn, suddenly we had to behave on court like convent girls at prayers. It was beyond a joke.

As the second half got underway, I loudly challenged her calls, giving her a lot of lip. I knew precisely how to be difficult and disruptive. Having no mainstay, no direction, no prospects, I saw no reason not to take it out on everyone, and Mrs Whitbread, the voice of authority, was a natural enemy. What I didn't know was that on the drive over to Culverhouse in the St Chad's minibus, Mrs Whitbread, who was shepherding a team of seven toughies, had kept hearing, 'I hope she isn't playing, Miss. I hope Fatima isn't playing. I hope she isn't playing, Miss.'

Mrs Whitbread was none too pleased when she found out that this Fatima was the one who kept disagreeing with her calls. I played netball the way, I later found out, she played hockey: aggressively, relentlessly, a bit of a killer. I myself was no mean hockey player either. As for netball, I wasn't a brilliant skills player, but I had a touch. I played Centre, which meant I was the fulcrum, the one who made the pace and who set up nearly every goal. Every moment of that match was cut and thrust, every goal hard-earned. Anyone could see that I knew how to read a netball game. They could also see that I knew how to open my vitriolic mouth.

But she wasn't taking anything off me. She wouldn't put up with my verbals at all. 'Stop giving stick to other players on your team, and stop querying my decisions,' she said in a voice loud enough to drown out fourteen players screaming on court and my own angry protest of innocence. 'Stop it, or I'll send you off the court. Now.'

I kept it down till near the end of the match when my temper reignited. Wanting to see what I could get away with, and wanting my team to win – it was a very close match – I questioned another of her calls. The umpire sounded her whistle and motioned to me to come over.

I wasn't going to go to her, and as Mrs Whitbread stared at me open-mouthed in disbelief, I held my nose in the air. One of her toughies, Donna Kempster, who played netball for St Chad's but played with me on the Thurrock Colts hockey team, tried to intervene. 'You'd better play along with her, Fatima, or she will ban you from the match. That's one teacher who usually means what she says.'

Impressed, I shut up for the remainder of the match. But my team didn't win. The match, which I wouldn't remember otherwise, was a draw – 16 all. It was also, I realised much much later, the turning point in my life.

Weeks later, on a Saturday afternoon when the girls on the Thurrock Colts hockey team found their match had been suddenly cancelled some of us, still in our gold jumpers and short black skirts, stayed on to watch the club's first team play. Mrs Babs Bannister, who managed the Colts and had stood up to Mrs Smith for me when I was late coming home from matches, was goalkeeper on the senior team.

During the warm-up one of the Thurrock players, whom I vaguely recognised, motioned to me, 'Keep your eyes on me,' she said, 'and you might learn a trick or two.'

The player was the very woman who had umpired the netball match. As the match wore on, I was impressed by the standard of her play, but what amazed me was that the woman who had told me to shut up on court now gave more stick to her team-mates and had more to say during the match than the other ten players put together.

Not long after, when I wanted to try the javelin, it was a sharp surprise to find out that this Mrs Margaret Whitbread was the

94

javelin coach at Blackshots playing fields, where the athletics club I belonged to, Thurrock Harriers, did their training.

At Blackshots, I suppose because I was known to be a trouble-maker, Margaret Whitbread seemed far from delighted to see me. But I kept coming back. If I wanted to learn to throw a javelin — and I did, the javelin was a magical implement — then I had to cope with her, outspoken and strict though she was, and she had to cope with me, a smart arse troublemaker. She began by taking me to one side and telling me very firmly I would be welcome in the javelin group only so long as I behaved. It was precisely the sort of school-teacherish threat that always got my back up and it came from a woman who as a player was a bit of a villain herself.

My answer to her, to my own amazement, was something in the order of, 'I'll behave, Miss.'

My friend Alma and I went to Blackshots twice in the week and every Sunday morning, going by bus on weekdays, but walking together to and from the track on a Sunday. It took a long time to walk but it saved our bus fares which we used to buy cigarettes. I had tried most sports on offer at Blackshots, finding the long, hard sessions at the athletics club a help in burning off the white-hot anger that was otherwise always with me. The coaches there were usually people I could get on with.

Margaret Callender Whitbread had grown up in Essex, the only child of a brawny chief petty officer who had boxed and played hockey for the navy and been an Amateur Boxing Association judge. Mrs Whitbread's mother, Marion, had sprinted for Essex way back in 1935. It was not surprising to anyone in that family that at sport Margaret was, as her father will tell you to this day, 'a natural'. His only disappointment was that she was not much of a boxer.

The sport she was passionate about was the javelin. Before marrying, she threw for England, continuing to coach even after bearing two sons. As an athletics international, she had travelled to glamorous cities all over Europe, and even to tiny, hard-to-pronounce towns, but she never won a major javelin championship, her best being at the 1958 Commonwealth Games in Cardiff, where, at the age of nineteen, she came fifth. She is still fond of Cardiff.

With no fanfare, no specialist coaching, no real reason to do or die, she had never reached the very top echelon of sport. Even so, sport was – as her husband John Whitbread, a tall, wiry docker liked to say, grinning from ear to ear – her second love, a close second too, but not too close for comfort. On Saturdays, in the afternoon, she played a game of county level hockey. But Saturday nights she was home with him.

At the height of her javelin career, she not only found that the Eastern Europeans had the world sewn-up, but that the other British thrower, Sue Platt, a professor's daughter, held the British record. At the 1960 Olympics in Rome Sue Platt would have won a silver medal, she made a tremendous throw, but she stepped over the line and the throw did not count. She was, in a way, to Margaret what Tessa Sanderson is to me, although they were never *bitter* rivals. They lost track of each other for over a quarter of a century, but when I broke the world record, Sue Platt sent a congratulatory telegram.

My own ambition to throw the javelin began, unlikely as it may seem, in a lesson at school. I am no scholar. Far from it. Sometimes I wish I were, but books have never gripped me. And to me, Greek mythology had mostly been something I had to sit through, if possible dozing quietly, before I was liberated by the bell to have my next game of netball or my next cigarette.

But the dramatic myth of Atalanta, whom no man could outrun except by cheating, and whose javelin had killed a horrible monster, made my eyes widen with wonder.

Atalanta had grown up like me without a normal family. Abandoned as a baby in the Arcadian wilderness and suckled by a female bear, Atalanta, none the less grew up to be a heroine, the greatest woman athlete of the ancient world. She was so gifted, so naturally able at sport, so fast a runner, that her reputation grew and her father claimed her back, demanding as was traditional, the right to choose her husband.

Atalanta was not at all eager to settle down. She liked her

freedom. A compromise was reached: she need only marry a man who could outrun her. Whoever did that would get riches too; but whoever challenged her and failed would die. Many tried and many died until one man arrived with a handful of golden apples, which he threw, one by one, across her path during their race. She kept stopping to see what they were and to pick them up, since they were golden. Not surprisingly, he won. These were devious tactics. He could never have won without distracting her. And dropping the golden apples wasn't even his own strategy – it was the goddess Aphrodite's idea.

What I relished in the story was the fact that Atalanta was a great female athlete who could not be beaten fairly. Her ability to triumph over monsters also appealed to me. My ambition was to be a great sportswoman like her. She had run, thrown and even distinguished herself as a wrestler – all Olympic sports in ancient Greece and at the modern Games.

As well as the inspiration of a great heroine from classical mythology, there was the living, breathing, shining example of Mary Peters, the hefty Olympic pentathlete from Belfast. In Munich in 1972, the summer after my eleventh birthday, Mary Peters not only won the gold medal, she also set a new world record. Because the pentathlon was five events in one, including running, jumping and throwing (the shot), Mary Peters had to train and train and train, building plenty of muscle on her sturdy frame. She was far from the traditionally feminine ideal, but nevertheless Mary Peters was a much loved, much admired British heroine. Like everyone else's in Britain, my eleven-year-old spirits had been lifted by her achievement.

The year before that, Princess Anne had won the European Championship! That was thrilling. Of course, there was no chance of my becoming a three-day eventer like Anne: I lived in the wrong world; almost everyone did. But it was possible for me to become an athlete.

What with one thing and another, particularly my luck in finding a coach, I began slowly but surely to focus on the javelin. I didn't really decide to take it seriously for quite a while though, but it was fun messing about.

Some credit for my choice of sport must go to the javelin itself. It is not only a magical event, it is a beautiful one. The flight of the javelin is a glorious sight, and, as I very soon discovered, letting go was a fantastic feeling. If only television used its nous and spliced the javelin competition together, showing it as a whole instead of in bitty, disjointed pieces, it would make transfixing viewing. You would feel the tension of the competition building and care, as I do, each time the javelin soars.

Even before I had acquired much skill, I loved the event, as my new coach certainly sensed. But if I really wanted to throw the javelin, Mrs Whitbread said, I must get my parents to buy me one and some proper javelin boots. I couldn't face telling her that I didn't have any parents, but I kept coming along to practice, albeit without the proper kit. Occasionally, she asked if I and my parents were still planning to get me the boots and javelin. My answer was always a vague nod.

When she found out that I lived in a home, she immediately gave me a pair of used javelin boots that she got from an athlete who had outgrown them, making a joke of the fact that the boots were hand-me-downs. 'They will be easier to break in.' The suede of which the boots were made was not as blue as it had been, and there were other signs of wear, but they were my first javelin boots. I was as excited, proud and happy as if they had come in a gift box from Harrod's. The boots were a little too big, but at Mrs Whitbread's suggestion, I stuffed the toes with paper and wore them.

And she gave me a javelin.

I was, if anything, even prouder of it.

Back at the home, the first person I saw was Ingrid, the German student who was working there for a year. Nothing would do, but I had to demonstrate my new javelin. It took me two throws up to the cabbage patch at the end of the garden, which is such a paltry distance I probably shouldn't admit it, even now. Ingrid politely oohed and ahhed.

One more throw, I said, retrieving the javelin. To my horror, the next throw was much longer than the others and sailed right through the French windows, landing with a loud tinkle of glass well inside the dining room. Fortunately there was no one in the room at the time.

Ingrid panicked. What would Mrs Smith say? I can't say I was Miss Cool myself. I hid my javelin in the closed cupboard near the back door – convenient for a quick get-away if necessary. When Mrs Smith returned, she was absolutely livid and, as soon as she heard it was Fatima, ignored Ingrid's explanation that it was an accident. Uncle Alan, she said, would see to me. I was sent to my room to wait until he had unloaded the car.

They had been away for the weekend at a house they owned in Aveley village, about twenty minutes drive from the home, and where they went frequently on what they called their weekends off. The fact is, I regarded them as my weekends off too. No aggro. No arguments. No bickering.

Now they were back and we were back to punishments as usual. My punishment, which I was called downstairs to hear, was that I could not go out after school for a month. That meant that javelin practice at Blackshots was off limits as was any visit to Auntie Rae. My pocket money was to be cut for one month to help to pay for the damage. Ingrid tried to speak on my behalf but they refused to listen to her.

Secretly, I did pop into Auntie Rae's anyway after school. Her house was near enough. But Blackshots was too far. Depressed and angry, I spent much of my extra free time smoking in the bathroom, putting my head out of the window to exhale the smoke.

So that Mrs Whitbread wouldn't wonder why I had defected as soon as I had got my boots and javelin, I decided to smuggle a note out to her. All I could find to write on was an airmail letter, which I stealthily removed from a cabinet in the dining room. The only place where there was enough privacy to write the note was the toilet. Not knowing her home address, I addressed the air letter to St Chad's School, where she read it in the staff room. Explaining that I had accidently hurled my javelin through the French windows and that I was being punished, I said that I hoped she would let me rejoin her javelin group when I could, because one day I was going to be the best javelin thrower in the world.

After what seemed long enough for the decline and fall of the Roman Empire to have happened twice, my term of punishment was over. This time Mrs Whitbread was pleased to see me. But there was no messing about. Like her star javelin thrower, a blond-haired, earnest young man called David Ottley, who was eventually to become the British record holder, I had to get right down to work on learning and honing my technique.

Just getting to grips with the javelin – learning how to hold it – was a matter of trial and a frustrating amount of error. There are three main grips: an index finger and thumb hold, a middle finger and index finger hold, and the one I use, in which my middle finger and thumb hold the javelin tightly behind the cord grip, while my index finger lightly (or not so lightly) folds around the shaft of the javelin. For further support, I wrap the rest of my fingers around the grip.

The run-up was the other headache. To throw, you run holding the javelin aloft until just before the line when you let it go. A good throw requires speed, rhythm and explosive release at the right moment. Put your toe over the line and your throw doesn't count. It has taken me years to develop this technique, and to this day I make little changes in the number of strides I take or the angle at which I hold the javelin. That first season, though, as I was a novice, Mrs Whitbread told me to have the front end of the javelin pointing slightly downwards. It made no sense to me, as I was trying to make the thing soar. But with Mrs Whitbread alternately coaxing me gently and screaming in my ear, I did as she said.

In July, when Auntie Rae came to see me compete at Blackshots, and when I won with a school record of 39 metres which still stands to this day, it was hard to tell who was prouder – her, Mrs Whitbread or me.

Then, after delicate negotiations, of which at the time I was entirely unaware, Mrs Smith agreed that I might have a meal at Mrs Whitbread's house in Chadwell St Mary, which was about twenty minutes drive away.

After javelin practice one afternoon, we got into her battered, mud-coloured Mini, and finally pulled up again after a circuitous ride which involved some screeching of brakes that gave me an inkling of why the Mini was battered. We were in the alleyway at the back of the two-storey, brick house. Walking past the modest back garden vegetable patch where the straggly green onions and yellowing parsley were in need of picking, I was brimming with anticipation. I had never before had a meal at teacher's house; never even been asked. And this teacher was more than a teacher. She was a coach, the best in all Essex, which so far as I was concerned meant the world.

As she began to unlock the back door, which was mostly glass, it was opened from inside by curly brown-haired Gregg, Mrs Whitbread's eldest son, who was four years old. His jovial nan had been looking after him and his brother Kirk, who was two and a half years younger, straight-haired and blonde. She was pleased we had arrived in good time because she was going out that night for a spot of old-time dancing.

While she and Mrs Whitbread were saying goodbye, I had a look around. Smaller than the children's home, their house was a bit bigger than Auntie Rae's house, and like hers had a homely atmosphere. There was a big, cheerful, gold dralon corner settee unit in the lounge and two matching easy chairs under a huge picture window. I plopped on to the settee and gazed out of the window at the small front lawn, which needed a mow, and the other houses in the street. I felt I could sit there forever.

But someone had to look after the boys while Mrs Whitbread prepared the tea. Playing piggyback in the garden with Gregg and Kirk was far from a chore, though, the three of us cavorting and giggling like three-year-olds, enjoying ourselves. When Mrs Whitbread's handsome husband John arrived home from the Purfleet docks the boys jumped happily into his arms. Hugging them warmly, John Whitbread, whose hair was the same brown as his son Gregg's, flashed me a friendly grin.

The five of us sat down at the kitchen table for tea. Putting a huge platter of ham salad on the green velour table cloth, Mrs Whitbread began to dish up. 'Would you like some beetroot, Fatima?' she asked.

'I'm not sure.' My cheeks flushed as red as the stuff on the table when I admitted hesitantly that I didn't know what beetroot was. We had never had it at the home.

'I suspect you may find you like it,' John Whitbread said. 'Would you like to try some?'

I did, and Mr Whitbread was right. I do like beetroot, although not the way I now like prawn cocktail, spaghetti bolognese, or roast beef amid mounds of Yorkshire pudding, all of which I had barely heard of and certainly never tasted at that time. It is hard to imagine now just how narrow my culinary and cultural horizons were, beetroot being only one of the countless things that were beyond my experience. Disadvantaged is precisely the right word for us children who grow up in institutions. But as I learned from John Whitbread, it is no embarrassment to encounter something for the first time. It can be an adventure.

Towards the end of the meal, during which there had been a lot of laughter, John said, in a voice that I suspected was teasing, 'Someone ought to warn Fatima about the queue. You do realise, don't you, Fatima, that there's a queue?'

'To do what?'

'To mow the front lawn. You'll have to fight it out with the other four or five girls who think they are teacher's pet,' he said with a smile.

'John!' his wife said.

'I'm only teasing the girl. And you. I can see she's a good sport.' To me he added, 'Margaret's a good teacher and as a coach she has to take an interest in her charges. At least she brought home a pretty one this time.'

There were many visits to the Whitbreads after that one, and much laughter and fun. The only sad part was having to go home. I had fallen in love with the Whitbread family and they had fallen in love with me. Even little Gregg felt the tie. One evening, as Margaret picked up the keys to the Mini and got up from the table to shuttle me back to the home, little Gregg told me what he had already told his parents, that he wanted me to become his big sister. Then he blurted out what he thought was a brilliant idea: why didn't they just buy me from the shop instead of borrowing me and having to return me at night?

But getting adopted wasn't that simple. No, not simple at all.

As a first step, the Whitbread family came to visit me at the home. Mr and Mrs Whitbread made certain they got on with Mrs Smith. Gregg and Kirk loved having so many children to play with, and the afternoon passed happily. But I felt sad for the young ones who lived at the home and who had to endure the moment of the boys' leaving to go home with their *mummy* and *daddy*. To those left behind it felt like a scab being pulled from a raw, festering wound. I could still remember the sharp, incomprehensible pain I had felt as a little one at being left on the shelf.

It had taken me thirteen years, but now I had found a family who had enough love in their hearts for another child. And they wanted me. It was little Gregg who had put the whole thing in motion when he found out that I didn't belong to a shop. 'I want Fatima to be my big sister,' he said.

As they crammed into the Mini, I wondered if I would ever get my dream.

'Be good,' Margaret Whitbread said. 'Try to stay out of trouble. That will help. But one way or another, John and I are going to get you out of here.' Immediately regretting that she had raised my hopes, she patted me on the shoulder and tried not to show her anxiety. Suppose they wouldn't let her foster me. Suppose something went wrong. So many things could.

My behaviour did improve, and Mrs Smith may well have wondered why it was that whatever Mrs Whitbread told me to do I would do quite happily, but if anyone else told me anything, I dug in like a donkey. Confirming that Mrs Smith had it in for me – and was never one to get things jogging along anyway – Auntie Rae quietly told Margaret Whitbread that to move mountains, in this case, it was best to start at the top. 'Ring head office,' she counselled.

Miss Toomey at head office, who didn't make the best of her looks but always took the trouble to say what she thought, was the one who put the show on the road. Things began to move quickly although Miss Toomey had warned there would be ages and stages and plenty of red tape. There had to be investigations, references, approvals by my social worker and by head office. But with Auntie Rae, unbeknownst to anyone, even me, giving Mrs Whitbread the gen behind the scenes, things began to gallop.

Since I was a ward of court, where I lived was ultimately up to the social services. But the woman who said she was my mother, whose consent would have made my new placement easier, banged down the telephone when Margaret Whitbread tried, at the social worker's suggestion, to talk to her. Then, when Adem came to the phone, he too was hostile. None the less, it was beginning to look like there was a good chance that true to her word Mrs Whitbread would get me out of there.

But there was another very worrying problem, as Mrs Smith took me aside one afternoon to explain. I will never forget sitting with her at the kitchen table that day, in one of our few moments of confidentiality, when she told me that if I went to live with the Whitbreads, if I allowed them to foster me, if I became a member of their family, I would be betraying Auntie Rae. How could I do such a thing to her?

The last thing I wanted was to hurt Auntie Rae who had kept me going for so long. Many times I had asked her to be my mum. She wanted to, but because of circumstances she couldn't. In the first place, there were only two bedrooms in her house, one for her and her husband, one for her son. The social services would not have countenanced my sharing with a boy. Now there was another fine woman willing to become my mum. But even though I yearned to move in with the Whitbread family and to become a part of it, I did not want to do it at the expense of wounding Auntie Rae. Sitting with my head in my hands, very near tears, I considered giving up all hope of adoption.

'You have to learn to think of other people,' Mrs Smith said, or words to that effect.

Then, whilst Mrs Smith sat in silence, letting what she had suggested to me sink in, and a tear spilled on to my cheek, Auntie Rae, whose shift was starting, sauntered in. Seeing the gloom, Auntie Rae said, 'What's this then?'

'A problem with Fatima, of course. I didn't want to tell you, but Maggie Whitbread wants to foster her.'

'Why that's wonderful.' Auntie Rae's face lit up with joy. 'Then she's been on to Miss Toomey like I suggested, and it's to go through.'

I have never in my life felt such relief. Mrs Smith had the decency to look embarrassed. I don't know what she had been playing at. I now found out how Auntie Rae had given Margaret Whitbread all the gen on how to arrange to foster me officially.

What happened next still makes me hurt whenever I think about it. Because of the social services, I almost didn't even get fostered. Even Miss Toomey, who was a caring woman, and who had no ulterior motive, tried to throw a spanner into the works. I'm sure she and my social worker Mr Walker meant well but they could easily have ruined my life. What happened was this. Bob Walker who really didn't know me or the Whitbreads that well told them that taking me into their home just wouldn't work because I had lived in children's homes for too long. He said I was too institutionalised for family life. That was 'the department's view'.

Even if I got along at the Whitbreads' at first, he predicted, 'the honeymoon period' would soon end. Then there would be unhappiness and heartache. Maybe even mayhem. Showing Mum the records of my case, he pointed out that my life had been a series of raised hopes and disappointments, which I had countered with hostility. I had a chip on my shoulder. The Smiths saw it and at school they were aware of it.

'But that's them, not John and me,' Margaret Whitbread said. 'I get problem children in my class all the time. Because they play up with another teacher doesn't mean they will play up with me.'

'It's not just another teacher,' he told her. My whole record was trouble.

Mrs Whitbread told him that all I needed was a family and I would be all right. Thank goodness she was a school teacher and *knew* that she knew children, or she might have been swayed by the 'authorities' who had read in some book that 'institutionalised' children could not adapt to family life and so wanted to deny me my chance.

Fostering a child usually takes longer than it took Margaret Whitbread. She harassed Mr Walker to finish his investigations of her and her husband's personal backgrounds so he could do his house visit quickly. To encourage him, she was often on to head office, where Miss Toomey was kindly but cautious. Meanwhile I had sneaked into the big pine bureau in the dining room where the case records of us children were kept and taken a look. I am not sure if they were the exact same papers that Margaret Whitbread was shown, but they told the same sad story. I remember dropping the pages, the facts of my case were so upsetting, and bending down quickly to gather them up before Mrs Smith or one of the others came in. They mentioned all the homes that I had lived in as a baby, as a toddler, as a child. I had never had a real home.

Just before the school summer holidays, the social services put their stamp of approval on my attending the one-week Guinness School of Sport at Crystal Palace, which Mrs Whitbread had recommended me for. She was now the British national javelin coach and had picked me as one of the promising young athletes to go on the sports skills course.

At last the personal investigation and references were deemed acceptable, so we were up to stage three: Bob Walker was coming down to 'inspect' the room they had for me. You had to have a room for the foster child – that was what had kept Auntie Rae from fostering me.

The room the Whitbreads had for me, as they knew only too well, was a problem. Not only was it minute, only six feet by nine, if that, but 'my room' was literally the vestibule which anyone entering the house by the back door walked through. And the back door was the one the family usually used because they could park the car behind the house.

Mrs Whitbread wrung her hands, knowing the social worker would be within his rights to say the room was unsuitable. But it was all they had. In their two-bedroomed house, the boys were sharing a room, sleeping on bunk beds. Mrs Whitbread and her friend Mrs Lynn Mays spent a whole weekend decorating my room, putting up pink velvet curtains and washing down the woodwork.

Margaret and John waited nervously for Bob Walker to arrive. Then they took him on a tour of the house, culminating with the tiny room. The house was tidy and spotless, not a fibre of the cream carpet out of place, and unnaturally quiet – the boys' grandad was looking after them at his place.

Taut and nervous, the tour completed, the Whitbreads led the social worker into the lounge and awaited his verdict on the little room. As he sat sifting through his briefcase, it was evident Bob Walker was not completely satisfied. Margaret Whitbread could not contain herself any longer. 'What's going to happen to Fatima?' Her voice was shrill with anxiety.

There was no immediate reply.

'Is the room, in your view, suitable?' John Whitbread asked quietly.

Ignoring the issue of the tiny room, Mr Walker said he was not at all certain they would be suitable foster parents.

Margaret gasped. 'But why?'

What he said, to their absolute astonishment to this day, was that there must be something wrong with the family because there were no family photographs on display. In fact, there was nothing on the walls but a clock. The family snapshots were kept in photo albums at grandad's. The Whitbreads had not been surprised when the social worker spoke again about it being too late for me to be adopted because – as he had told them before – in his opinion, I was too institutionalised. But photos on the wall?

Evidently, he was going by the book – some textbook he must have read as a student and taken all too literally. Margaret and John proceeded to tell Bob Walker exactly what they thought of him.

'I have had enough of petty bureaucracy,' John said. 'The child needs a home. We have one for her.'

'It's ridiculous for Fatima to be subjected to the Smiths,' Margaret said, 'when there is a loving home she can go to.'

There was much more of the same, quite a heated discussion.

Picking up his briefcase, Mr Walker said he could see that they were concerned. He would consult with head office and inform them of the social services' decision just as soon as he could.

After two weeks of anxiety, there was a semi-happy ending. The Whitbreads were told that I would be allowed to spend the school summer holidays with them on 'trial'. Margaret Whitbread's answer was, 'Absolutely not'. She and John felt it would distress me too much to feel 'on trial'. No matter what, they would make it work – both knew how desperate I felt about further rejection. And they were confident all would be well. The social worker still felt I was unsuitable for family life.

The best they could get from head office was the agreement that I move in with the family for a holiday but that after three weeks, Miss Toomey, Mr Walker, and their boss Mr Butcher, who was very experienced, would meet with Mrs Smith and Mrs Whitbread. Once again there would be a summit to decide my fate.

Rushing home on the last day of school, I picked up my few belongings which I had already packed the night before and, with my friend Alma to see me off, I danced back to school. I had arranged with Margaret Whitbread that she collect me there on that sunny day, 25 July 1975, because I didn't want to be met at the home.

Alma was a little sorry to see me go, but she was happy for me. As we got near school, she looked off the other way and said, 'I'll miss you, Fats.'

'Alma, I'll miss you too.' My voice cracked. 'You know I will.'

Then we hugged each other, right there on the way to the school.

As we arrived, a few minutes early, I saw Mrs Whitbread's Mini turn the corner and pull up with a screech, making me glad we were not quite there waiting. Hugging Alma once more, I got into the car.

'Everything OK?' Margaret Whitbread asked.

'Yes, Mum.' I grinned.

'Not Mum,' she said gently. 'Not yet. We've got to get past that meeting with head office. But don't worry. If anyone can do it, we will.'

'I know,' I said, repeating silently, 'I know, Mum.' It didn't matter to me that I was still Fatima from the children's home and she was Mrs Whitbread, I knew that she was eventually going to be my mum. But she didn't want to hurt me by counting our chickens before they had hatched. Suppose at that meeting with head office something went wrong! My heart nearly stopped at the thought of it, and my hand went to my mouth.

Flicking a glance at me as she drove, Margaret Whitbread said firmly, 'Fatima, everything will be all right.'

I nodded. It *had* to be all right. I would think on the bright side, which was as glittery as a diamond tiara: that very night I would be sleeping in my own bed in my own room in the Whitbread family house. The thought of it made me feel jubilant. All the way to Chadwell St Mary I kept on grinning. I couldn't stop smiling, I was so happy.

When we got to the house, the boys couldn't stop holding my hands and giving me a kiss. I had presents for each of them, a gleaming black model of the John Player Special Grand Prix racing car for Gregg and a bright plastic London Red Bus for Kirk. When John Whitbread came home from work, he hugged me. Then we all sat down – Mum and Dad, my two brothers, and me – to have our evening meal.

That weekend we went to the family caravan at Creek-Sea for a two-week holiday. The eight-berth caravan seemed to me to have every possible mod-con – flush toilet, electricity, TV, etc. – yet it was in the middle of the country with a spectacular view of the River Crouch. We took bikes with us, played croquet, marbles, darts, cricket, badminton, tennis and bowls. We went swimming, on outings to Malden, to the Southend Festival and walked along the seashore. We seemed to have time to do everything.

Fishing was the best. My father and brothers and I would sit beside the lake for hours waiting for a bite. There were other fishermen dotted about, quite a number of them, sitting in rapt silence. The lake was peaceful. But growing restless one morning, I climbed up to the little footbridge about a hundred yards away, and cast my line. I got a bite almost immediately. The boys were thrilled and screams of excitement echoed around the site, which the other fishermen did not appreciate because it scared the fish away; or so they believed. Dad and I got a few more nibbles and more cheers from the boys, who even pulled in a couple of carp and some eels themselves. Try telling children to keep the noise down when they are holding a wet wriggling fish. The boys got to throw the small ones back into the lake and this to them was a great treat.

After what was our first family holiday – and it had been a roaring success – Mum and I took off for Crystal Palace, the national sports centre on the outskirts of London. There, Mum was to be one of the coaches for the seven days of the Guinness School of Sport, which was offering intensive training in all Olympic sports. I was one of the trainee athletes.

I'll never forget my first impression of Crystal Palace. The grass seemed to be greener and the playing fields bigger than any I had ever seen. Not only that, there was a new tartan track. You could have floated a javelin on my enthusiasm. Not just mine. The fine young athletes created a perennial high. But exciting though it was to live in the dormitory with the others, to eat meals with them, to train together till the sweat became a salty river running down our necks; satisfying though it was to learn some new skills and to hone others, pleased though I was at that, what I really wanted right then, more than anything, was to be living with my new family in my new home.

That I would ever be able to do so on a permanent basis was by no means certain, of course. The big meeting with Mr Walker, Mrs Smith and head office was looming. After we had been at Crystal Palace for a few days, Margaret Whitbread asked the other coach, Maria Birdwhistle, to keep an eye on me because she was off to the children's home for the meeting.

I was very nervous. So, as Mum told me later, was she. When she got to the home, fortunately it was Auntie Rae who opened the door. She gave Mum a warm drink and some confidence. The social workers had not arrived yet.

Eventually they did. Then, without further ado, Bob Walker, Miss Toomey and Mr Butcher, a top man from head office, sat down with Mum and Mrs Smith to decide my fate. Mrs Smith made it more than plain that she felt I should stay at the home. This was odd to say the least. For years, it had been clear to Auntie Rae and me, even to Edna and to casual visitors like the Thurrock

Colts' manager, Babs Bannister, that Mrs Smith had little or no love in her heart for me. In fact, she appeared to regard me as a festering thorn in her side. The year before Mrs Smith had pressed for me to be moved to London. Now that a family wanted me, she was insisting I stay at the home. It made no sense.

Miss Toomey said that the social services were in the middle. They had to do what was best for everyone concerned. Of course, they were pleased for Fatima, but concerned that Margaret and John Whitbread might be making a mistake.

'Fatima is at a difficult age,' Miss Toomey said. 'And you and your husband have two young sons. It could possibly be too much to handle.'

'John and I know what we can handle. Fatima likes being in our family.'

'Yes, you're getting on well now, but even someone as experienced as Mrs Smith has had problems with Fatima. What concerns me is what will happen when the "honeymoon period" is over. It could get rather nasty. You and your husband might find you no longer want her and she will begin to feel about you the way she feels about the Smiths.'

Years later, Mum told me that at that moment she almost took a punch at Miss Toomey. But instead she said, as calmly as possible, 'We know what we're getting into. As I told you before she came to live with us a month ago. We want Fatima. We still want Fatima. We will always want Fatima no matter how naughty or troublesome she is. I know what Fatima can get up to. John knows. But we love her and want her as our daughter. Our sons love her. It will be cruel to take her away from us and bring her back here where she has been so unhappy. It will be cruel to her.' Mum almost couldn't go on. 'And cruel to us.'

'Being emotional isn't really what we're here for,' one of the three social workers in the room said.

'Isn't it?' said Margaret Whitbread. 'A girl's future is at stake. Her whole life.'

'We do understand that,' another of them said.

Then Mr Butcher, the top man from head office, put in another word on the Whitbreads' behalf. His words carried the day. It was decided there and then that I could stay permanently.

In one final effort to jeopardise my future – or so it seemed and in light of what happened still seems to Mum and me – Mrs Smith said that she wanted me at least to spend the last week of the summer holiday at the home, just so I could experience living there again and see if I really did prefer to be part of a family.

Mum objected, but Mr Butcher thought it a fair compromise. In view of Mrs Smith's long-standing service – in view of everything she had done for me over the years – coming back to live there for a week was, he thought, a way I could say 'thank you'. The idea of it still makes me want to spit.

Mum drove home to Chadwell St Mary to tell the boys and Dad that I was going to live with them permanently. They were very happy and excited. To Dad, alone, she explained that there was a 'clause' to the agreement. After the Crystal Palace course finished, I would come to live with them permanently but at the very end of the summer, I was to have a final week's 'holiday' at the children's home.

'More red tape,' Dad said angrily. 'It will choke Fatima. It is down to us to make certain somehow that it doesn't choke her to death.'

It was a few days later, on our journey home to Chadwell St Mary after the Guinness School had finished, that Mum told me about the clause.

'I'll never go back there. I hate it there. I'm not ever going back to the home. Why should I!' I cried.

In a very calming voice, Mum tried to explain that if I didn't, it would probably jeopardise any future with them. I felt very sick inside. Mum did too, and nervous lest during the week at the home I would be upset to the point of being difficult, so difficult that I might jeopardise my future.

In the week leading up to my return to the children's home I cried a lot if I was on my own for any period of time. My friend Alma came to visit at the house for a day, and she told me to buck up, I could do it, and we had a good time making terrible remarks to each other about Mrs Smith.

The day came for me to go back to the home, a Saturday

morning; I would be back at the Whitbreads' the following Friday night. The whole family was very, very upset, but Mum and Dad told me it would be the last time we would be apart. They reminded me I had Auntie Rae who was on my side living just around the corner and that I could ring them and reverse the charges on the telephone whenever I wanted.

As I got out of the car at the home — I wouldn't let Mum accompany me inside. She said to me, 'Fatima, just remember two things: that we love you and that it is very important that this week you behave.'

The Smiths were not even there when I arrived. The student on duty couldn't understand why I had come back. No one had told her. The Smiths were away for the weekend at their house. I phoned home. 'The Smiths aren't here. You can come and get me.'

Mum said I must stay in case they were just out. 'They're away for the weekend.' But Mum said she couldn't come for me, much as she wanted to, because it was a head office decision that I stay a week and we must abide by it. She tried to play it down, but I could see she couldn't understand either why the Smiths were missing. Auntie Rae said it was a scandal but that we should look on the bright side. If the Smiths were not around, I wouldn't have any arguments with them. 'Count your blessings, Fats,' she said, ruffling my hair.

The Smiths returned on the Sunday afternoon. Ignoring me, they went straight to their room until later that evening. When I rang to tell Mum, she said I should just amuse myself and not misbehave, reiterating that no matter what, we had to abide by the head office decision.

Throughout the week the Smiths more or less pretended I wasn't there. To be more exact, they were cool, barely civil, even at times hostile. I remember phoning Mum every day and telling her I didn't see any point in staying. But by then I knew I had to stick it out.

On the last day I went outside to sit on the fence and wait for Mum. I sat, my legs dangling, almost a nervous wreck when Mum screeched up to the kerb. She had come, with the boys, to take me home. While Gregg and Kirk played on the swings, Mum and

I had a last chat in the garden with Auntie Rae.

The Smiths had gone out. Auntie Rae was appalled that they had made no effort to see me off even though I had given them the pound of flesh they wanted. 'You were good and brave to stay the week, Fats,' Auntie Rae said. She said again how happy she was for me. She even thanked Mum for giving me the family I had always wanted.

Then it was time to go. As we Whitbreads piled into the Mini, Auntie gave me a big smacker of a kiss and told me to get on with my new life. Margaret Whitbread put her key in the ignition and turned over the engine.

'Off we go,' she said to me. 'Ready?'

'Ready.'

'Do you want to take a last look?'

'I've seen too much of the place already. Let's go.'

She stepped on the pedal, and we were off. I was fourteen years old, and I knew I was going to become a Whitbread. The elation I felt is impossible to describe adequately. Never had I felt so joyous. It was the most important thing that had ever happened to me and despite all the wonderful and terrible things that have happened since, it still is. No one can ever take that moment of joy away from me. Nor can anyone top it. For almost the first time in my life, the gods had smiled on me, and they were grinning ear to ear.

I had had to wait until I was fourteen to get what most people have from the start — a family. But at last the heartbreak of not belonging anywhere was over. No longer was I an unwanted stray at the pound. At last I had found a mother — and a father and two brothers, even a grandad and a nan.

10

The Big Wide World

Happy families are all alike, with birthdays to celebrate and holidays to go on and little jokes which make every member of the family career with laughter but leave the rest of the world wondering what on earth was so funny about that. Life at the Whitbreads' was ordinary life. It was wonderful. I ironed Dad's shirts. I cooked meals for the family whenever Mum was working – she didn't mind one bit; she hates cooking, and I adore it.

Every meal was an adventure; often as not I was cooking something I had never eaten before. It would be a couple of years before I got to the point of perfecting recipes – I had so many basics just to try out. But my spaghetti bolognese is as good almost as you get in Italy. I've never been to Bologna, but I can speak for Rome.

When I had first come to stay with them, I mean before Crystal Palace, when Mum was still insisting I call her Maggie because the social services had not said I could live with the family permanently, Mum bought me a brown leather jacket. It was something I had wanted ever since junior school, a fabulous soft, leather jacket with a good quality zip, roomy pockets, and the height of fashion. It was warm too. I wore it with a green polo neck that it set off, and thought I looked stunning.

I wore that outfit for days at a time which was a bit of a problem because it was really too warm to wear indoors, and unless there was a family outing I rarely went out, even to school. I so loved being in my family's home, I didn't want to leave it. How different the word 'home' felt on my tongue and in my heart when it meant

115

the house I lived in with my family, not the children's home, which was merely an institution, not a home at all.

My friend Jill Burroughs, a heavy, large-boned sprinter with fine, straight, dark hair, trained with me at the local track, but we both played truant from school. Sipping coffee with Jill and dragging on a cigarette was far more stimulating than some of the lessons at my school. But in the main Jill and I must have been the most wholesome truants in the world. When we skipped school she would happily sit there watching, or even help me bustle about the Whitbread kitchen, baking cakes as a surprise for the family. Or I would iron the boys' fancy T-shirts. Batman, Robin Hood and *Startrek*, in those wee sizes, made me smile each time I smoothed them into place on the ironing board. This was more ironing than the Whitbreads were used to, and once it was even too much: I burned a hole in my father's shirt. Not certain how he would react, I got into a state, which Dad couldn't understand the reason for at all. 'But it was an accident, wasn't it?' he said.

The only screaming and shouting came when we both began to play cowboys with the boys, who were being Indians that day.

I loved the boys. Their little faces always lit up when they saw me. My bigger one glowed too. I taught the boys to swim. They taught me the role of big sister. In the mornings they would wake me up with their favourite new game called 'Jump on Fatima'. Mum would get Gregg off to school and I might take little Kirk to nursery school on my bicycle. On Saturdays, I chaperoned them to the matinees at the cinema. As often as possible I sat on one of their bunk beds, listening with rapt attention to their record books of *Thomas the Tank Engine* and *Jungle Book*.

When five-year-old Gregg started having sleepless nights and on school mornings started to look as worried as a stockbroker on the day of the Big Bang, his teacher confided to me that a boy in the class above Gregg was bullying him. Big sister intervened in a rather different way than a big brother would have. A big brother would have threatened the bully or punched him here and there. I urged Gregg, who was shivering in his grey school shorts at the thought, to go up to the bully and warn him bluntly that if he didn't desist, Gregg would hit back. It may be that my scowling face helped, or it may just have been Gregg's bravery, but that was the end of it.

I was still having fearful nightmares too, and would awaken sobbing and terrified. The man ringing the chain became ever more menacing. Mum or Dad would come into my room and sit with me late into the night, listening and comforting me as I revealed all the things that had happened to me before I came to them. Happy though I was in that family, it took a long time for the nightmares to stop being a regular occurrence. Now, it is only occasionally that I have that dream of the man in the cloak and wake up terrified.

I remember mostly the joy, the novelty of feeling safe, but recently Mum told me I was so disturbed that it was a major problem for a while. And when I think about it, I realise that it has really taken until the last three years for me to feel totally secure. Until then, some small, scared part of me still believed that one day I would wake up and the Whitbread family would have disappeared, leaving me to return to somewhere as bad as the home.

My period of adjustment to family life was also hampered by two external problems. Firstly, going to a new senior school where everyone else had already established cliques was no pleasure. One or two students made certain it wasn't. And, secondly, I was mortified when Aliya's half-brothers made a special trip to Essex from London and turned up at school threatening to destroy my new-found happiness with the Whitbreads. After quite a nasty scene, they were ejected by the headmaster, leaving a sour taste.

Although I had been rebelling against whomever was in authority since well before my teens, I was so pleased at having parents at last, that I have never had any of the usual set-tos with them. We have had our ups and downs, like any family, but no major battles. Family life was to me sweetness and light, peaches and cream, lovey-dovey stuff. Perfect.

When dad came in unexpectedly and smelled cigarette smoke, he didn't make a scene, but told Mum. Little by little I was weaned from the weed. When I burned the steak, there was no to-do about it. We all ate up, and they even complimented me on my cooking.

117

Except for those nightmares and my own occasional bursts of temper, it was a placid life. How I loved my new family! What I had expected in a family was a fantasy of perfection, a kind of Cinderella's dream. It was very unlikely that I would ever get such a thing or that such a family as I imagined even existed. Yet I had found it. I felt in the first months that I lived in Chadwell St Mary that getting a family, getting this family, was the most important thing that had ever happened to me. I still do.

I've had my share of life's ups and downs, as the Gladys Knight song, the *Best Thing That Ever Happened To Me*, says. Whenever I hear that tune, I call out to the boys, or my father, or Mum, for them to listen — as they do for me. It's a comforting song.

All was relatively blissful until Mum received a phone call from my deputy headmistress to find out why I was never at school. Mum told her the truth: that I liked it at home.

'She'll have to come to school, Margaret. It's the law.'

I went in for a day or two, now and then.

The deputy head persisted. She felt it was important, especially as I had had perfect attendance at my previous school. But what really got me back to school was the lure of sport. One day as I was ironing, and my friend Jill folding the laundry, we decided that we were going to play county hockey. The way to do that was to come up from the school hockey team.

Without much difficulty we made the school team. In fact, I got selected for most of the school teams. My pride of achievement was dampened just a bit when one or two people goaded me, saying I had no right to the place because I had not been at Torells from the first year. One of them got quite nasty. I will never forget her saying, 'We don't want you at this school, Paki.'

It was the first time in my life, I had ever been the butt of a racial slur. And when the girl shouted 'Paki' at me, I almost turned my head to see if she was talking to someone else. I had never thought of myself as coloured; and I had always thought of myself as thoroughly British.

Outspoken Miss Bullock, the sports teacher, told me not to

European champion, West Germany, 1986.

(ABOVE) Wearing my favourite necklace.

(OPPOSITE) In the back garden with Mum and my brothers and the Mayor and Mayoress of Grays, Thurrock, who presented me with a decanter and glasses after Stuttgart, 1986. [*Alex Strachan*]

(ABOVE) My godson Boyd, aged two and a half, at his home in Upminster, 1986.

(OPPOSITE) Mum and Dad at home, 1988.

World Championships, Rome 1987.
World champion.

(ABOVE) I had to bite my gold medal to believe it was real. [*Associated Press*]

(OPPOSITE ABOVE) One bonus for winning the World Championships and part of the fun of being on Wogan was a sizeable cheque towards Olympic training.

(OPPOSITE BELOW) I also enjoy presenting trophies, here to the winner of the Krypton Factor International prize, 1987.

National Westminster Bank PLC
9 SEPTEMBER 87
Pay BAAB TRUST FUND re: FATIMA WHITBREAD or order
FIVE THOUSAND POUNDS ONLY £5,000.00
THE TIMES/MINET SUPREME AWARD
MINET GROUP SERVICES LTD

The wiggle, 1988. [*Sun*]

(OPPOSITE ABOVE) At a reception at Number 10, Nigel Mansell and I met Mrs Thatcher, November 1987. [*Press Association*]

(OPPOSITE BELOW) Holding the award for Sports Personality of the Year 1987. [*Press Association*]

One of my favourite dresses.
[*Sun*]

(ABOVE) At the Tilbury Docks near home, 1988.

(OPPOSITE) I won the World Championships with a Sandvik javelin like this one.

With my wax portrait figure at Madame Tussaud's. [*Madame Tussaud's Ltd*]

worry, that they were jealous of my considerable talent. I had never thought of my ability at sport as a talent until then. Nor had I realised it was 'considerable'. That sounded serious. As for the aggro in the gym, what I could do to help her and the situation, Miss Bullock said, was to avoid fights even when someone else was picking them. Holding my temper back wasn't always easy, but I tried. As for playing on every team at school worth playing on, I entirely stood my ground.

Eventually, though, it had to happen. Things boiled over when one of the girls who had made unpleasant comments, approached me fiercely at practice on the school pitch. I pushed her away roughly. We ended up in a fist fight, Miss Bullock having to part us. In the changing room after practice, Miss Bullock threatened to drop us both from the team. The other girl blurted out, 'But it's not fair for Fatima to play for the school when she's just arrived here.'

'On the contrary,' replied Miss Bullock, 'because Fatima certainly isn't eligible to play for some other school, is she?'

If either of us wanted to continue on the netball team, Miss Bullock said, we had to shake hands and get on with it. That girl and I became reasonably good friends after that, and Torells won the league.

The day that Virginia Wade won Wimbledon and restored British pride, I was awarded the Victorix Ludorum at the 1977 District Schools Championship, having won four events, the maximum. My triumph was not reported in headlines or on television. It mattered only to my family, teachers, to my opponents and to a few friends. Yet my joy and pride of accomplishment may well have been as great as Virginia Wade's, and her Wimbledon victory fired my imagination. If only, like her, I couldn't help thinking, I might some day win something that excited the whole nation!

Unlike Virginia, I could not put my kit in the washing machine and otherwise rest on the Sunday. I was scheduled to compete at Crystal Palace stadium in the Southern Counties Championship.

Mum, who had wanted to watch me and Wimbledon, had instead been asked at the last minute to take a two-woman team, consisting of the sprinter Andrea Lynch and Tessa Sanderson, Britain's javelin thrower *extraordinare*, to an invitational meeting in Düsseldorf, and then to take Andrea on to Rome.

In Düsseldorf, the stands were full of servicemen who had driven over from their bases to watch a star-studded cast of athletes: Ed Moses, Don Quarrie and Kathy Schmidt, the American javelin thrower who later that year set a world record. Mum, who was team manager, shared a room with Tessa. They got on well. Tessa, the Jamaica-born Brummie whom everyone in Britain was beginning to hear of, scored an impressive triumph, not only setting a new British record of 64.42 metres but also defeating two top throwers, the East German Marion Becker who was now West German and Kathy Schmidt. Tessa's was no mean feat because these two were the reigning silver and bronze Olympic medallists.

Tessa already had her eye on the 1980 Olympics. No one considered she could be threatened in any way. Certainly not Mum. Least of all Tessa. After the meeting, when Mum mentioned in passing that her daughter Fatima, who was five years younger than Tessa, was coming up and that she had talent and might one day be a danger, Tessa laughed. Mum shrugged, 'It's years off anyway.'

Tessa flew back to England, victorious, and Mum and Andrea went on to Rome. As they settled in, Mum told her that I was competing at Crystal Palace that day. Andrea said, 'Go and watch her win. I'll be all right on my own.'

There was no space on the flights from Rome, and as I discovered a couple of days later, Mum took whatever flight was going, arriving at Heathrow via Copenhagen and Brussels rather late. She drove non-stop to Crystal Palace, which is nearer London's other airport, Gatwick, and arrived at a trot as I was warming up.

'You're back, Mum.' I was so pleased.

'It wasn't difficult to arrange,' Mum said.

She hoped I wasn't too tired — competing back to back is not ideal. But having her there boosted my morale so much that any trace of tiredness evaporated. I went on to win the competition, the culmination of a fine 1977 season.

Mum told me she had never before had so dedicated a young athlete to coach. Never had I felt dedicated to any task as much as I did to winning with my javelin. Deciding to become a full-time athlete, I left school with my parents' blessing. With my mother-coach behind me, I began the journey that I hoped would take me to the top of the javelin world.

Becoming an athlete is an expensive process. Just paying the food bills can be ruinous. Thank goodness that early on a meat packers decided to sponsor me with monthly deliveries of their product. Steaks, legs of lamb, chops – they were full of protein, which I needed lots of to build muscle. Sport makes you ravenous. The great Ben Johnson who exploded out of the blocks to a new 100 metres world record of 9.83 seconds in Rome, outracing the legendary Carl Lewis, is always hungry. People who knew him as a lad remember him having a gargantuan appetite. The world middle-weight judo champion Neil Adams has told me that when he first came down to London from Coventry, in the late 1970s, there were times when the bottles of milk left outside his neighbours' front doors were too big a temptation to pass up. Neil, who never stole anything in his life, couldn't help uncapping a bottle, throwing his head back, and gulping the entire contents down.

Living with my family, it never came to that. There was always milk in the fridge and plenty of food on the table. Even though they were not rich and had two growing boys, there was never any pressure put on me to contribute money to the housekeeping.

It is well known in sports circles that many young athletes live on the dole. Some start training to get over the boredom of no job, and some have no job because they are so busy and so tired after training. I never went on the dole. I don't begrudge the others, not at all, but it just wouldn't have felt right for me.

My high hopes of going to Canada on the 1978 Commonwealth team faded when less than a week before the trials, which were in Birmingham, I came down with tonsillitis. To say I was feeling under par on the day of the meeting would be an understatement. But I had to compete to qualify for the Commonwealth. Mum drove me to Birmingham, and I threw badly. To my relief, the doyenne of women's athletics, Marea Hartman, who has been around a long time, and the other selectors took into account my competitive record, which was superior to the competitors who out-threw me in Birmingham. I would go to Canada.

Tessa Sanderson, who was my inspiration and whom I was just getting to know, was going as the British number one. I was the number two. I was eighteen, she was twenty-three. In the run-up to the Commonwealth, we both took part in a couple of internationals, one of them in Strasburg, an elegant old city with a magnificent ancient cathedral. Regardless of religion, even if they don't have a religion, people stand gazing up at the cathedral in awe.

In Strasburg, I shared a room with Tessa. When she is in high spirits, Tessa can be silly with the best of them and great fun. We had a lot of laughs, the loudest being a slightly unkind one during the competition and at the expense of our hosts the French. One of the French throwers, who shall remain nameless, was making Tessa edgy because she was using Tessa's personal javelin, which the rules allowed. Using Tessa's javelin, the girl made what looked to be her best throw ever and a new French record. The girl watched the javelin land and elatedly jumped up and down. As the French officials ran on to the field to measure the distance, Tessa yelled at the girl, 'Go and fetch my javelin back.' Not thinking, the girl dashed over the foul line to retrieve the javelin. The French officials paid no attention and began to measure the throw.

'That counts as a no throw,' Tessa said. 'She shouldn't have stepped over the line. They are not going to measure that.'

Together we began pulling at the tape, shouting as loud as we could, 'That's a no throw.' After a few minutes of uproar the officials finally accepted that technically the French thrower had fouled the line. I don't know if it was gamesmanship on Tessa's part or just the French woman's bad luck. Tessa, by the way, was winning anyway, and there was no hope of a medal for me. It was just one of those things I am not entirely proud of, but rules are rules.

Before the Commonwealth Games there was one other international, at Crystal Palace. In addition to the javelin, I put in a spot of hurdling when the girl on our team had to drop out. If I finished the race it would mean one more British point. I went to the line-up, and as I stood on the track, waiting for the start, the world record holder from Poland, Grazyna Rabsztyn, who was in the next lane, leaned over and mustering her English, informed me, 'You have the wrong spikes on.'

I didn't possess a pair of track spikes so I had to hurdle in my cumbersome javelin boots. They didn't win me the race, but we made our point. At the dinner-disco that night where I danced and danced, I paused to receive the Outstanding Female of the Match award. I hadn't won the hurdles, but the extra effort I had made in taking part in the race had won me that. I remember having a lot of fun at the disco.

At last the Commonwealth Games.

In Canada, I roomed with Tessa again. In the mornings, we used to go out on bikes, cycling around the town. In the evenings, before the competition, we went to the disco. We danced, danced, danced, with lads of all nations.

All the British hopes were pinned on Tessa – I was still up and coming. She was reaching her peak. On the day, she won with a modest throw of 61.34 metres, three metres less than her British record, and even further short of the Olympic, European and Kathy Schmidt's 69.32-metre world record. There was not much competition in the Commonwealth. None the less, Tessa and the tabloids were delighted. And I was actually pleased with sixth place and 49 metres.

It was at those games that one of the other athletes told me that Tony Duffy, the well-known sports photographer, wanted to meet me. Could I meet him for a coffee and a chat in the village cafeteria?

Intrigued, I went to the cafeteria at the appointed time. I found our conversation to be interesting and sensed that he was rather smitten with me. But I couldn't really believe it, as he was so much older than me, so much more sophisticated. I was a girl; he a mature man, twenty years older than me.

Not long after I got home from Canada, Tony, who was the

founder of Allsport, the pre-eminent sports photo agency, phoned Mum to suggest he photograph me. Many of the shots, he said, would find their way into the media.

The photo session was to be at Crystal Palace. Daley Thompson, who was at Crystal Palace training, decided to sit in on it. So did the javelin thrower who has since become a friend, Peter Yates. During the photo session, they made some choice comments, but Tony Duffy, frowning with concentration, seemed oblivious. He had me pose in positions which emphasised my figure, and at that particular time in my young life I was rather well endowed, with a certain amount of puppy fat. At each new pose, Daley and Peter would make some new rude, sniggering remark and ogle me.

The photo session lasted three hours, and as I was rather naive, it was only much later that I realised that it was unusually long.

When we adjourned to the cafeteria for a cup of tea, Daley and Peter tagged along. There, Daley said more than once, that he hoped Tony was paying me for the session. Daley kept on in this manner, pointing out that Tony would make money from the pictures and therefore I should get some of the benefit. Daley went on and on in this way. Tony, who has ginger hair and a fair complexion, flushed. But Daley kept niggling him.

Finally I told Daley to shut up, as Tony was going to ensure that I received media recognition. I liked and admired Tony, and when he invited me to Shaun Pickering's birthday party, I accepted. Shaun, who was a British international, is the son of sports presenter Ron Pickering. It was a glittering occasion, the first such I had ever attended. Many sports personalities were present, including Daley and the then current lady in his life, the swimmer Sharron Davies.

Mary Rand, whom I met there, said she remembered my mother competing and warmly wished me luck. But she was surprised and, I could see, disapproving, when she realised I was at the party with Tony Duffy. Later I found out that she was worried that he would take advantage of my inexperience and youth and persuade me to pose for provocative photos. But he was throughout a gentleman.

Everything that winter went precisely as it should have. Mum and I were beginning to think I might even hope for a medal at the 1979 European Junior Championships coming up that summer.

Then on a damp, foggy morning at Crystal Palace, where the international squad was training, one of the younger coaches made us train vigorously indoors where it was warm, and afterwards go outside immediately and start to throw. Too inexperienced to remember that damp weather means danger, he gave us no warning against throwing flat out straight away. And I, equally inexperienced, gave it my all.

On virtually my first throw, I hurt my back and had to lie down in my room. At lunchtime Mum, who had been coaching another group of throwers, and I popped into the physiotherapist who was attached to the course. We were relieved to hear that he was confident that I would be all right in a couple of days. I had merely overstretched.

But the next morning my back was so painful that Mum took me to the casualty department of our local hospital. The X-ray showed that I had fractured a vertebra.

For the next eight weeks the pain was so sharp that I couldn't even bend across the bath to turn the taps on. It was all I could do to swim, which I did at the modern Blackshots swimming baths. But even getting to the baths was a major achievement. First putting my trusty tan-coloured orthopaedic pillow on to the driver's seat of our car (I had been driving since the age of seventeen), I would ease in and then gently place the pillow in position in the small of my back. Just getting in and out of the car was exhausting. I could barely take care of myself and was of no help to anyone else in the family. I felt useless.

When I resumed training after nearly two months 'holiday' all I could manage was some very lightweight working out while sitting in a chair and a speck of jogging. The first time I tried the javelin I couldn't throw more than 30 metres without feeling pain. Mum suggested that I leave throwing alone for a while, limiting myself to repetitions of the javelin action from a bench.

The intensity of the pain ebbed and flowed, depending on how hard I used the shoulder which wasn't healing as it should. Even

125

a shrug could elicit sharp pain. Nothing or no one could conquer the agony. Not physios, doctors, nor acupuncturists, and none of the experts could say with certainty when I would get over the injury, which I continued to aggravate by competing.

There was no proof anyway that desisting from sport, giving up, retiring from the javelin almost before I had begun, would make the injury go away. The damaged vertebra had healed with adhesions of gristle around it. Even having heat treatment and manipulation every day hadn't stopped the pain. The injury hurt me most when I threw and it reduced the range of movement I had in my shoulder. It would have been a good excuse for giving up competition. But it wouldn't have been the answer.

To be honest, at the time, it didn't even occur to me to retire. That just wasn't one of the options before me. Cutting myself off from competition, almost before I had begun, would have been like cutting off a limb. You amputate when you have to. But only when you have to.

There was, as I say, no proof that retiring would help. And if I was staying in the sport – and I was – I had to compete. Competing, as I had by now learned, is practically the only time you throw flat-out; in practice you take fewer chances, holding something in reserve. But you can't ever be razor-sharp without competing. You can't win if you don't throw.

There's a lot to that old saying: 'No pain, no gain'.

Three months after Margaret Thatcher had become Britain's first female prime minister, I found myself in a sleepy little Polish industrial town near Auschwitz. It was a place called Bydgoszcz – we Brits immediately renamed it 'By Gosh' – and it was the site of the European Junior Championships. I was a very young eighteen-year-old when it came to international competition, not much on from brand new, and I was certainly not likely to win the competition on that sweltering summer's day, 19 August 1979.

I was grateful for the good luck card that Tony Duffy had sent me, but I knew that no British girl had ever made the final for a throwing event in these championships, which were open to under nineteen-year-olds. No British woman in history had ever succeeded in winning a throwing event in any major European competition, not even Tessa, the Commonwealth champion. Because the Eastern Europeans and the Finns took the javelin so seriously, the standard in Europe was far higher than in the Commonwealth. State-aid, sports science, and every facility had been there for the women behind the Iron Curtain.

Having made the final, despite all the training days lost to injury, I awoke on the morning of the competition with my stomach aflutter, and even Mum's constant chatter couldn't keep my mind off the coming competition. In fact, I could tell by all her prattle that she was wound up tighter even than me. Breakfast was a few crumbs of toast and a spoonful of boiled egg. I was too nervous for more: my stomach in knots.

We took the team coach to the stadium. All those smiling British faces made me feel more confident. But entering the changing room, my face fell. The massive East German thrower, Katrin Strobel, was already in her blue vest and white shorts. At nearly six foot, she towered over my five feet four and a half. As I smoothed on my white vest and white shorts and began to pull on my red GB tracksuit, the chunky Soviet champion, Natalya Rula, arrived. Her best throw was over 60 metres, dwarfing if not making a mockery of my best of 56 metres.

The bubbly, dark-haired Bulgarian Antoanetta Todorova, who was nearly a year younger than me, but far more accomplished – I was a fan – was there too. With all the Eastern Europeans surrounding her, she might easily have ignored me, but Todorova smiled and said, in her thick Slavic accent, a few words that were intelligible as a welcome.

Banter in half a dozen languages filled the changing room as each and every athlete tried to relay a sense of confidence she didn't feel. The close escape of the day before, when I had almost decided to withdraw, made me even edgier than I might otherwise have been. Mum and I had found, to our amazement, that the Poles didn't have any Apollo javelins. According to international rules, the full range of javelins commonly in use should be available at a major championship like this one. But the only Apollo in

Bydgoszcz, I was told, was the one I had brought along for informal practice.

This was a blow. I didn't want to start learning to use another sort of javelin in the midst of the European Junior Championships. Thankfully, Sir Arthur Gold, who was so influential in international athletics was at the stadium. After a long conversation in which I explained to him about the javelins and after he had then consulted his committee, he came back to say if I was prepared to sell my virtually new Apollo to the Polish Youth Federation for a nominal fee, the javelin would be made available for me and all the other competitors. I was paid the grand sum of one Polish zloty.

Then, with the Apollo, I qualified, which was why I was sitting in the changing room with the cream of Eastern Europe. But I was not in the best of moods, and when Strobel gave me a long stare, I was sure she was sneering.

Outside, in the stadium where dozens of athletes, not just in the javelin, were stretching, jogging on the spot and taking little practice throws, it was chaos. I did a few stretches, but after nearly being hit by a stray javelin, I knew I needed a quiet place to warm up.

Wearing my red and blue GB tracksuit, I walked a fair distance with my coach, Mum, stopping at a small grassy area near the railway line. Then I jogged off to do some striding and stretching. But I soon came jogging back. 'Mum,' I said, 'My back hurts and my stomach is still a wreck and Strobel thinks I'm less than nothing.' Becoming more and more agitated, I began to rattle off anything and everything worrying that came into my head. I was a tangle of nerves.

Mum just chatted away to me about the wind, which was getting a little stronger and how that might affect the javelin.

'You aren't even listening, Mum,' I was annoyed. 'Everything is terrible and you don't even ...'

Mum interrupted sharply: 'You are only going to throw in a competition, Fatima. Not that many years ago, more than a million Jews were packed into the trains that ran on this railway, and travelled past this very spot to Auschwitz, to their deaths. That is

128

something to be upset about. Competing in a championship is not. Fatima, you can only do what you can do.'

Pulled up short, I nodded.

'But, Fatima,' Mum added, lest I mistake her meaning. 'You've worked hard. Give it everything you've got.'

We walked together back to the reporting area. Then, just before she had to leave me to it, she said, 'Good Luck'.

I would need it.

Before the real throwing starts, you get a few warm-up throws. There, on the Tartan javelin runway was Katrin Strobel taking a throw with my Apollo javelin. Then she ran and collected the javelin, to have another go. If I wanted to use the Apollo, that was my problem. She wasn't letting go. This sort of psyching out, I would soon learn, was common enough at big meets. Muscle is only half of winning; mind is the other half. An athlete who 'feels' is not going to win. After her next throw, I made certain I got to the javelin before she did. But when I picked it up, she tried to take it from me. I wouldn't let go. Why should I?

'Clear off,' I said. 'It's my go.'

'*Nein*, I throw now.' She gave a tug on the javelin, to pull it out of my hand.

'Leave off.' I gave a yank back. 'It's *my* javelin.'

'I throw now.' It was turning into a tug of war.

Pulling on the javelin, I said defiantly, 'Me first!'

Strobel began shouting in German and I in English, neither understanding the other, but getting each other's meaning, and neither of us willing to let go. Each of us had one hand on the javelin now. I clenched my other fist. Seeing me do it, Strobel, surprised, backed off momentarily. In that moment, I gave a decisive yank and walked off with the javelin.

I had won that battle, but what about the war?

Glaring at her when she took the javelin for her first throw of the competition. I realised that now she was barely even noticing me. Her mind had switched focus entirely to concentrate intensely on the athletic feat she was about to perform. I watched with trepidation and some admiration as Katrin Strobel thundered up the runway, unleashing a lightning bolt that soared 56.02 metres.

That was a fine opener, only a few centimetres below my best so far.

The three other throwers who preceded me came nowhere near 56 metres. I didn't expect to win the competition. How could I? But I would break my back before I would let the European Junior Championship title, a coveted title, go to that vindictive East German. I gave my opener everything I had. It landed, exactly like Strobel's, at 56.02.

Things hotted up in the third round. The talented and good-natured Bulgarian, Antoanetta Todorova, threw 57.58, which Strobel topped with 58.02. Now Strobel, remembering me, did a little war dance of delight, and raised her arms over her head in victory.

But the cardinal rule of competition is that you don't put a medal around your neck until you have won it. It is not only bad form, but it may lead to defeat. It made me angry to see Strobel lording it over all of us like that. Who did she think she was? Snatching the javelin from the stand, I strode back to the Tartan runway for my throw, tension and anger in every pore.

Mum in the stands was chain-smoking and muttering under her breath, 'Relax, relax. Remember your technique.' When I looked to the stands, I couldn't find her. But I heard the British 200 metres runner Mike MacFarlane call out clearly, 'Come on, Fatima.'

I took a deep breath and let the tension flow out of me, like water through a colander, Mum's favourite analogy. I looked down the red Tartan runway to the green field beyond which was dotted with tiny markers where I would have to throw my javelin. It was just like the field in Essex where I practised, just like the field where I had won my first school title, the same day that Virginia Wade had won at Wimbledon. It was almost home.

Wrapping my mind round the javelin, visualising the perfect shot, one in which every muscle was instructed correctly and did as it was told, I held the javelin aloft and began to run. Then, whipping my arm forward, I let the javelin go.

The roar from the British contingent massaged the spasm of pain I felt from my damaged vertebra. The scoreboard was flashing 58.20 metres. I was in the lead.

The pride of East Germany looked personally injured. She was not the champion's champion her brawny predecessor the great Ruth Fuchs had been. Nor was she an admirable competitor like Petra Felke, who would later inherit the East German mantle and become my great and respected opponent, and a friend. No, Strobel seemed to me to be a vindictive soul. But she had the stature and the muscle to win. She had expected to win. She had been told that she would win. And she certainly did not expect to lose to a Westerner.

Her face showed such dismay that I could imagine what must be going through her mind. Something in the order of: 'The cheats, they have kept that British midget under wraps — but at least I am ahead of the Russian and the Bulgarian.' At that moment inside her head, Strobel settled for second place. There were two more rounds of throwing, but the competition was effectively over. It was just as well. My back was stiff. By the next round it was aching cement.

A few hours later, at the medals ceremony, as the band struck up the British National Anthem, the gold medal was placed around my neck. I had become the first British woman to win the European Junior Championship. Beating the best of Eastern Europe in my age group — and as everyone knew, Eastern Europe were the best in the world — I had entered the record books on an important page. I was elated. And I was proud. And I was grateful to my coach, Mum, who had taught me more than technique. As I stood there on the victory rostrum, grinning, the lights on the scoreboard read for all to see,

MISTRZOSTWA EUROPY JUNIOROV —
FATIMA WHITBREAD

Shortly after my return from Poland, Tony Duffy arranged to photograph me with my medal. He was encouraging me to document my sports career with photographs, which he so rightly said, would make the great moments come alive for me again and again.

On the phone he told me the photos were great and he would send me some. Instead, he turned up in Essex. Mum invited him in for a cup of tea, and he sat down to wait until I got home from training. I was delighted at the photographs, but hesitant when he invited me to a ball at the Savoy. It was to be a big occasion, with many stars. Tony said it would be a good introduction into the world I would have to get to know if I became a champion. In consultation with Mum, I decided to go.

To me the Grand Savoy seemed a palace. Mum and I had taken a lot of time choosing my dress, a fabulous red one with a halter neckline. Tony told me I was a knock-out.

Geoff Capes, the shotputter who had been my 'big brother' in sport since my international debut, was there. I went over to talk to him, but when Geoff realised Tony was my escort, he went into a rage. I could not understand Geoff's reaction and was upset. But all in all I had a fine evening, dancing and dancing.

I saw a bit more of Tony, and I liked him, but I didn't want to get seriously involved with him, and said as much. In answer, he asked me out to dinner. I was taken aback, but he said I really had to go, as he had a surprise for me. He arrived with a box of chocolates, which I thought was the surprise. But during dinner, he handed me a small parcel.

'It's for you, Fatima,' Tony said. 'Open it.'

Carefully unwrapping the little package, I found a beautiful ruby ring in the shape of a heart.

'I hope it fits,' he said. 'Try it on.'

I put the ring on the fourth finger of my right hand. As he had guessed my size, the ring was just a little too big.

'What a wonderful present, Tony,' I said. I thought it a lovely, generous gift.

Much to my astonishment and dismay I soon read about the ring in a magazine article that said I was engaged to a sports photographer. It was a cheek. I phoned Tony up straight away and told him off. 'You can have your ring,' I said.

Tony apologised. He said he would rather I kept the ring as it was only a token of his affection.

In 1980 I was awarded one of the Winston Churchill travel fellowships, available to British sportsmen and sportswomen. I chose to go to Gibraltar. The whole family went with me. Unfortunately, Tony got wind of it, and turned up 'on assignment' in

Gibraltar where he was a nuisance, not just to me but to all of us. By this time I had met someone else whom I kept in touch with by post.

Later that year I competed in Japan and China, at the Eight Nations Games, and Tony turned up again, on assignment. I was not pleased to see him. I tried to tell him gently that his attentions were unwanted, but I couldn't seem to make him understand. Meanwhile, I longed to see the man I was beginning to care more and more about, and who was in Britain.

Tony meant well of course. He was and is sincere. But his persistence was getting me down. I discussed the matter with one of the other athletes, Meg Richie, with whom I was rooming on the tour. Meg, seeing that I was at my wit's end, took it upon herself to tell Tony in no uncertain terms to leave me alone.

To his credit, despite his infatuation, he backed off, though we remained friends. Because he was a sports photographer, our paths still crossed from time to time, and he sent the occasional postcard from far away places.

11

My Dearest Friend

On 2 April 1982 Argentinian invaders overwhelmed a garrison of eighty-four British marines. The Falklands War began, and the man I loved went out to fight it. I had known him for nearly two years, seeing him only from time to time because I kept having to train or to travel to compete and he went wherever the army sent him.

But I had begun to allow myself to think that he and I had a future together. When I was supposed to be lifting weights in the garage near home where I did my training, or on a flight to a European competition, I would find myself daydreaming about living with him in our own flat, then in our own house with a couple of little ones who had Steve's firm chin and laughing blue eyes or his sturdy physique. Because of the army, he was nearly as fit as I was.

Ours was a light-hearted relationship, but one full of tenderness and joy. Steve — that is not his real name, but I will call him that — meant a great deal to me, even though the way we met was most inauspicious. It was not at a ball or at Buckingham Palace. Not even an introduction by a friend.

Like many young soldiers who had seen my picture in the newspapers, Steve wrote to me in the summer of 1980, after the Moscow Olympics, where I had been a flop. Until bags of post from the British people began to arrive, I had thought of my dismal performance in Moscow as only a private mishap, an embarrassing detour on my climb towards the summit of athletic achievement.

Even going to Moscow, I had begun to think, before the letters arrived, had been a mistake. I had been selected just by the skin of my javelin, if you will, because after winning in Poland, my

134

back condition had deteriorated, becoming extremely painful and seriously affecting my performance. This time even the physio didn't seem to help. What I did was all I was capable of. I trimmed my training and competitions programmes down to the bone. By making a monumental effort whenever I did compete, I made just good enough a showing to be selected for the Olympics – with one proviso. I would have to pass a fitness test at Crystal Palace.

I well remember covertly gritting my teeth, trying not to let the pain show, as I threw for the two British Board officials, John Le Masurier and Andy Norman, who supervised my fitness test. My trial throws were in excess of the qualifying standard so they told me to go home and pack my bags ready for Moscow.

Mum and Dad and the boys were so proud that I was going. Mum had never been to the Olympics. She might have gone to Rome in 1960, along with her rival Sue Platt, but a groin injury kept her off the team.

I did not expect to win, of course, not at my first Games, but getting an early introduction to the Olympic fanfare and tension would be an investment for the future. It was Tessa who was the British hope.

I found Moscow very drab and the food was awful. And for Tessa and me the Games were a disaster. My back hurt. She was all nerves. And in the qualifying round I threw a bit better than she did. But there was no comfort in that, my throw was abysmal. Neither Tessa nor I threw well enough to qualify for the Olympic final.

I was disappointed not to qualify: angry at myself and sad. But my sense of sorrow was nothing compared to Sebastian Coe's. When I went to visit him in his Moscow hotel room late on the morning after he won silver behind his rival Steve Ovett in the Olympic 800 metres, missing gold by five-tenths of second, no one was there besides Peter Coe, his father who was also his coach. Losers don't get many visitors. That's the only advantage of losing: you find out who your real friends are. At the time, I was less a friend than a great admirer of Seb's ability and achievement as an athlete.

I went, knowing he would be somewhat upset, to offer a few

words of comfort and to tell him everyone who mattered knew he was a champion anyway and that he would soon show the others. When Peter Coe let me into the room I got a shock. Seb was lying on his rumpled bed still in his pyjamas, crying his eyes out. I didn't stay long. I had never yet gone out expecting to win and failed, so I had not realised how much it could hurt to lose.

Later that week when he won gold in the 1,500 metres in Olympic record time and Ovett had to settle for bronze, Seb cheered up.

What helped soothe my disappointment was the letters. A crusty old highlander wrote on lined paper from Scotland to say that it was only the Olympics, not a death in the family, and that I should cheer up, adding that her heartfelt wishes were with me for the future. Children wrote; and men who preferred football and rugby, some of whom admitted that they couldn't even throw a dart. They all said they would be rooting for me whenever I threw the javelin, adding that I should keep it up, for Britain. I hadn't realised before that other people cared anything at all about what happened to me in the future or were cheered by my prospects.

Young men of my age wrote too, often requesting a glamour shot. I sent Steve the one of me in a bikini entering the sea. He wrote back thanking me just before I left for China and Japan to attend the Eight Nations Competition, where I came sixth.

Three weeks later, when I returned, there were two letters from him waiting, telling me who he was and how pleased he was to be writing to me. I remember chuckling when he described all the ways the army has of getting fit and keeping fit. 'Chinnies' 100 at a time, and 'burpes', all the usual, and every day. And of course, being in the army, he ran with a heavy, bulging pack on his back.

For a few months we wrote to each other, casual letters, this and that, nothing cataclysmic. But I liked the sound of him. One morning the telephone rang, and when I picked it up I could hear pips. Steve, ringing from a call box, wondered how I was – and if sometime he might come and see me.

'Yes. Why not?'

'Well,' and he hesitated. 'How about today? I'm in Kent. I could be there in little more than an hour.'

I gave him some instructions to direct him on his way.

At about one in the afternoon Mum and I were sprawled on the floor, head to head, going over some training instructions she had written out for me, when I saw a broad-shouldered, young man with wavy, chestnut hair and a cute, pert nose approaching the front door. He was wearing civilian clothes. Smiling at me through the picture window, Steve knocked on the porch door. Even before he handed me a box of chocolates and gave me a peck on the cheek, I liked the look of him.

Over a cup of tea in the kitchen we sat for an hour chatting about anything and everything. Mum and my brothers said hello and he was pleased to meet them, especially the boys. There was no one thing, no memorable moment, but the time went very quickly. I liked the way he absent-mindedly fingered the cuff of his pale blue shirt when he was asking questions about me. I liked the way he smiled at me over his mug of tea. And his voice. It was not at all gruff but it was soothing, except when he was laughing. Then it was fun. I liked being with him. I found him to be a very nice person. Sometimes you just take to someone. I took to him.

At three p.m., though, I had to go training. 'If you don't go now, Steve,' I looked at my watch, 'you will be overstaying your welcome.' I was going running, up One Tree Hill. Steve offered to drive me there and back.

'I have an hour's training to do. You won't get impatient?'

'I won't get impatient.'

One Tree Hill is very steep and slippery, and especially when damp, as it was, is impossible to run up without spikes. Steve stood at the bottom of the slope, watching me run up and walk down, run up and walk down, over and over. I was doing three sets of four repetitions each up that hill which was a distance of about 150 metres. Trying to build up aerobic endurance, stamina, more even than speed, with Steve watching and calling out encouragement, I had to put in a proper run every time. He was good for my training.

After each run, as I walked down the hill with my eyes glued to him, I felt a warmth in his smile. And every so often he asked me how many more there were. On the last one he decided to race me to the top.

Taking off his jacket and rolling his trousers up so that they wouldn't get muddy, he was getting into position when I said, suddenly, 'Go!', and sped up the hill. He had to chase me up the steep slope, which would have been a killer if he hadn't been fit. Although Steve was wearing street shoes, he was as competitive as I am, and he caught up with me. But there was no way I would let him get by.

In a big burst of effort to beat me at the last, Steve pounded forward, but his feet slipped out from under him. I heard a plop and then a laugh.

Craning my neck, I saw him sliding, on his way back down. He looked so funny I couldn't stop laughing. Running back down to make certain Steve was all right, I saw that he was embarrassed and amused at the same time, and didn't at all mind my laughter.

It may have been then that we fell in love. Yes, I think it was then.

Laughter and love were what our relationship was about. But this was not even properly our first date. We moved cautiously. In the car, after chatting me up some more, Steve said softly, 'I have enjoyed myself meeting you. And I think you have too, Fatima. Can we meet again – soon?'

A week later, on a Saturday afternoon, we were strolling together past the Tower of London. Walking, talking, hand in hand, on one of those perfect London days when the sun never seems likely to set and the city seems so romantic, we strolled along the Thames Embankment all the way to Blackfriars. Then, as we paused to gaze at the river, Steve, suddenly realising we were going to be late, hailed a taxi to take us to *The Mouse Trap*, Agatha Christie's play, which was on in the West End. We rushed into our seats in the stalls, sitting down just as the curtain was going up.

No wonder *The Mouse Trap* has broken the world record when it comes to the number of West End performances – about thirty years of them. It has a clever twist. The first act made us hungry and we ate sweets during the interval. After the theatre we went for a meal. I can remember feeling very happy and content to be in his company. My feelings were already quite strong towards him, and his eyes were looking at me lovingly. Near the end of the meal, Steve told me he was going to Kenya.

'Thanks for giving me the elbow. Nice knowing you,' I said tartly, upset that there were to be no more wonderful evenings.

'Don't be so silly, Fatima.' He reached across the table and took both my hands in his. 'I will just be away for a while. I have to go. This isn't the end of us. We've only just begun.'

My heart began to fill with happiness. I had become so attached so quickly. Almost from the moment I saw him striding up to my front door, there had been a magic, a spark between us. I felt happy in his company. I could see he felt happy in mine. But, I realised with a start that I was scheduled to go to the USA for a month's training a few days before he got back. I felt a pang of foreboding. It seemed as though circumstances were always going to be against us.

Still holding on to my hands, Steve said, 'We will just have to look at the stars at night wherever we are, because the stars are the same the world round. That will bring us together until we can be together.'

In California I trained hard and well. The whole family had come along, including grandad and nan. We were having a great time, but occasionally I couldn't help thinking how it would be if Steve were with us. I often found myself looking up at the stars and realising how much I missed this man I hardly knew.

Much later, months later, when we met again, at the Tower, almost the first words Steve said were, 'Is there anyone else?'

'There's no one else.'

'Then,' his voice went all shy, 'Would you be my lady?'

'Yes,' I said, feeling shy too, 'I'll be your lady.'

Again we made a day of it, walking hand in hand, browsing in the shops, seeing a movie, eating. Like me, Steve was always hungry. As the meal was ending, as we sat sipping our coffee, Steve handed me a Carpenters greatest hits cassette he had brought for me. Very softly, he began to sing to me the tune he regarded

139

as the best and most apt track: *We've Only Just Begun.*

You could have used my smile as a torch, it was so bright. After that, I never seemed to be able to get him out of my mind. Nor did I want to. Just thinking about him, about us, cheered me immensely.

Driving out to the family caravan in the Essex countryside on the first of our many visits, both of us in high spirits, Steve and I sang along with the Carpenters' tape on the cassette recorder. Compared to his clear, strong baritone, my voice was a shrill squawk. He sang *We've Only Just Begun* to me over and over. It was our song. *Top of the World* was his other favourite. 'That one is your song,' he said, predicting that as an athlete I would top the world.

Steve, who had no doubts at all of his masculinity, felt my sports career was no threat and was keen for me to do well. His greeting when we met always included the words, 'Have you done your training?' I didn't let him know how much seeing him did interfere with training because he was prouder even than I was of my athletics career, although it had only just started to get off the ground. But there was no doubt at all that in my heart athletics took second place to him.

The caravan site, which was near Burnham-on-Crouch, was quiet and peaceful since the summer season was over, and there was no one there except us. It was to this caravan that we had gone on holiday as a family when I first became a Whitbread. Originally the caravan had belonged to grandad, Mum's dad, but he had given it to us. I had Mum's permission to go there with Steve, but my father, who wouldn't have approved even though I was nineteen years old, was none the wiser.

The setting was lovely, in woodland right near the River Crouch and that little lake where Dad and the boys and I used to go fishing. There was a panorama of trees, but we were in a grassy clearing which trapped whatever sunlight there was. There were always squirrels playing nearby and rabbits running in the distance. But Steve and I had no distractions from each other except the ones we wanted.

Breakfast was always fresh eggs from the local farm with

fresh bread and milk which Steve had driven to Burnham to get. Sometimes we played short tennis, sometimes we cycled into Burnham and sat for a long time on the harbour wall, dangling our legs in unison and chatting with the seagulls.

I will never forget the time we arrived at the caravan on a perfect afternoon and wanted to have a picnic but the grass was too high. We found a mower.

I always took my running kit with me and he took a pair of trainers and shorts. Our running sessions, sometimes quite arduous ones, would end up with a game of hide and seek. Knowing the terrain better, I would dart behind a tree and as he passed jump out at him. It would end up with laughter and cuddles and kisses. We did all the young, foolish things that you do.

In his company I felt pleasure and joy, I felt relaxed and ecstatic, I felt the usual things but they were not usual to me. Anything and everything made us laugh. I often thought I was dreaming, a happy dream at last, one I never wanted to wake up from. He had made me come alive.

He told me that he loved me, and I loved him very much.

When I went off to Cyprus again for spring training, our plan was to spend a couple of days together at the caravan when I got back.

In Cyprus the Falklands flare-up was in all the papers. Everyone thought it would blow over. Instead, the shooting war started. I still really did not appreciate what was going on. Nor, I think, did Steve. Never did either of us think that his unit would go there — unless he was keeping it from me.

When I came home from Cyprus I was looking forward to seeing him, but two days before we were to meet, he sent a letter saying his leave was cancelled. His regiment was to undergo two weeks of intensive training and then they were going to the Falklands. It was a complete shock. To comfort me, he said, 'It won't be for long. At most a few months.'

Then, by telephone, he asked me to see him off. 'If you don't want to go, I'll understand,' he said, 'because it will be an awkward journey and you won't be able to tell which one is me.'

'Of course I'll come, Steve,' I said. 'I want to.'

'Even though I won't see you, it will be nice knowing you are there.'

Mum accompanied me because I needed moral support and a navigator. Leaving Chadwell St Mary in the early hours of the morning, we arrived in Southampton a bit before six a.m. I still hoped there would be a moment to give him a quick cuddle and a kiss.

The noise of the harbour was incredible – loud martial music, marching soldiers' feet, so many people calling out 'goodbye' to passing soldiers, so many people crying. They marched past and on to the ships, regiment by regiment. We could pick his regiment out, but not him. I not only didn't get to see him at close quarters, I didn't see him at all, but I just kept waving all the time in case he spotted me.

When the ship pulled away I felt empty and afraid.

I am not a great newspaper reader, but I examined the papers carefully every day. And I listened to the war news on television and on the radio. If I heard any of our records, I just cried. I prayed to God to keep him safe.

One morning when I opened the newspaper I was shocked to see his name printed there. I had never expected to read it in the list of the dead, just a name, a statistic. You can imagine how hard that was to come to terms with. The shock, the anguish. He was such an alive person, and he meant the world to me. I was devastated.

I still sometimes ask myself why he had to be one of the 252 British fighting men who died in the Falklands. Why him? Why us?

All I had left were the letters he had sent me, a tidy stack of them with my name in his small, neat handwriting on the square white envelopes. From time to time I would take them out of the drawer to reread and gaze at the snapshots I had, one of him and a few of the two of us which we had taken in a coin-operated photo machine. My thoughts would turn to what might have been.

But I knew I had to live in the present, and I had to stop reopening the wound, feeling the sharp pain of loss. I knew I had to get on with my life. And I couldn't do it if I kept reading his words and looking at his face. Four years after his death I made the decision to stop, and I did it the only way I could. I ripped them all up, the letters, the photographs. You can't keep reading the same letter, and looking at someone's face when fate has decreed it isn't to be.

It was time to let the wound heal as well as it ever could. I know if Steve had lived, my life would have been quite different. I might have had little ones by now and never have become world champion. Or, with his encouragement, I might have had both. More than six years have gone by since he was wrenched away. That's a long time. I've learned to live with the fact that it is a part of my life that will always mean something to me but which is over. But I lost a little something of myself when I lost him.

I am putting our story in my book to pay tribute to Steve. I have not given his real name to spare his family, whose grief would be rekindled and who would have to bear the indignity of notoriety. I have, in my time, had unscrupulous reporters camped on my doorstep. I don't want to do that to them. I never knew them when he was alive. I don't feel I have the right to force myself upon them now that he is gone, especially so much after the fact. But I loved their son. He was joyful, exuberant, sensitive, my dearest friend. A loving, caring man. I'm sure they know that.

I still mourn his death, the death of a dear friend. As I sit here, a woman of twenty-seven, who has travelled, seen much, done much, felt much, I feel that deep inside me there is a place that has been touched and never will be touched again. Of course I have dated other men, even really cared about one of them, but I often think of Steve and our times together even now, and it is a long time later.

I knew I would miss him, and I do.

12

Coming of Age

Miserable though I was in the weeks after Steve was killed in the Falklands, I decided to compete during the summer season. What better way to drown my sorrow than by immersing myself totally in my sport? He had always wanted me to be top of the world. I would do it now. For him. For me. To hold on to life.

Only time would soothe my grief, but I could deflect it. Dedicating myself to athletics, which was all I had left, I focussed all my hope, all my need, all my energy and intensity on the javelin. Slowly, I began to make progress.

In sweltering Athens in September 1982, I qualified for the final of the European Championship. Immediately, I went to the telephone and rang Mum in England, beseeching her to come to the final which was the next day. I knew I would need moral support. The *crème de la crème* of the javelin world was competing. It was going to be tough. I would have to get some sleep and I was having frightening nightmares again. The man in the dark cloak was tolling the bell once more.

Mum moved mountains to join me in Greece. The headmaster at her school gave her special permission to take a brief, sudden leave. Dad, who is wonderful, took two days off work to look after the boys. Mum arrived at about one a.m., and we went right to sleep so that we could get up early. There was no chance that I would win anything, but I wanted her there, seeing what was clearly going to be a blue riband competition and rooting for me so that I could do my best.

I threw a very creditable 65.62 metres, but in that company it was only good enough for eighth place. The victor was the Greek

144

Anna Verouli, who had suddenly, suspiciously, blazed like a meteor on to the javelin scene. Her winning throw was a then rather phenomenal 70.02 metres. Her compatriot won bronze. Whereas my own years of hard training had failed to pay off with a major medal – Mum had warned me that the build-up would take years – the Greeks had had a swift and unexpected rise to prominence in the javelin. There were rumours that anabolic steroids were the reason why.

It is unlikely that, if she had been there, Tessa Sanderson could have done better than Anna. Tessa, though still regarded as the top British thrower, missed those championships because she had had a freak accident. During a gentle club race, she fell, not only landing on the elbow of her left arm, which cracked, but ripping her Achilles' tendon. I felt sorry for Tessa. That wasn't an injury anyone would wish on their greatest enemy, which she wasn't. She was only my greatest rival. There is a slight difference, a matter of respect.

Her injury also kept Tessa out of the 1982 Commonwealth Games in Brisbane a month later. But I went. After the Europeans, those Commonwealths were almost a doddle. We had no throwers of the quality of the Europeans. The gold medal throw was a metre less than my sixth place in Athens. None the less, on that Australian day, I could manage only bronze.

But I knew I was maturing as a javelin thrower. That same year I went to Bratislava, Czechoslovakia, seeking top class competition against the East Europeans and the Cubans. I found it in the shape of the reigning Olympic champion, Maria Colon of Cuba, of whom I do not have fond memories.

To rattle me, she and her compatriot, Vila, would walk across the runway just as I was preparing to throw. Her gamesmanship went even further. Every javelin thrower puts down a little marker at crucial points of the runway to indicate the stages of her run-up. For each competitor the position of the marker is different because it depends on your stride and pace. Maria Colon kept removing my markers. I was angry, but I kept control of my emotions, and defeated the Olympic champion.

The following season Tessa had recovered and, supposedly, as good as new, was going to Helsinki for the first ever World Athletics Championships. But there seemed to be no reason at all for me to travel all the way to Finland, as I was physically sapped by a severe tonsil infection – not tonsillitis, but something the doctor said was worse, a related condition called quinzies.

I knew if I didn't go to the Worlds, I wouldn't be missed. But equally, as I realised at the very last minute, I would be shattered if I missed them. Getting up from my sickbed, I flew with Mum to Helsinki, arriving well after the games had started, but before the javelin competition. Because they no longer expected me to turn up, I discovered when I got there, that my room at the official athletes' village had been allocated to someone else.

So I shared Mum's hotel room. It was quieter in the city than in the village. There were no late parties; nor did I have to contend with the moods of other athletes. Their depression in defeat which could be contagious and their nerves before a competition when they feared defeat. Most of the athletes at any competition were losers. The winners were too few for their elation to rub off.

The relative solitude was helping me concentrate. The money we had to pay out in Finnish markkas for the hotel room and meals seemed a fortune at the time – I was not yet anywhere near receiving £10,000 a meeting in subvention money which I was later to receive for some appearances. But the savings were immense when you calculated the effect on my inner resources. It was because there was no room at the inn, if you will, that I discovered, by accident, the benefits of staying outside the village, as a few other athletes did, mostly the stars.

And, of course, you see more of a place. I will never forget going into a local restaurant for a meal and noticing with pleasure there were javelins as decoration on the wall, instead of wine bottles or photographs of footballers.

Like the Eastern Europeans, the Finns take the javelin very seriously as a sport. To this day, no one has matched Matti Jarvinen, the Finn who reset the men's world record ten times in the 1930s and won the European title twice. Finland has a historic gallery of javelin stars up to and including the reigning men's Olympic champion, lanky Arto Harkonen.

146

When I arrived in Helsinki, I was a virtual nobody in javelin terms. Years of work by Mum and me had paid off, but not very dramatically. In the four years since my victory in the juniors in Poland, my throws had steadily got better, but as a senior, I had failed utterly to establish myself on the world stage. Since I had no reputation to uphold, I was delighted just to be competing in those inaugural championships. Since that season I had been throwing 69s, it was my secret hope to take home a bronze medal. But there was only an outside chance.

I nearly blew it in the qualifying round, and barely scraped into the final, qualifying twelfth, in the last and least position. Part of it was due to feeling under par. Much of it was jaggling nerves.

After that poor showing everyone thought I was entirely out of the running. There was no pressure on me at all. Not a hint of it. What I was doing in Helsinki, all I could be expected to do, was chalk up experience for the future.

Nevertheless, when I walked out on to the Tartan runway to take my first throw of the six-round competition, I gave it everything I had. You don't hold back. You dig deep. You have to give 100 per cent if you ever expect to be a champion. I neither saw nor heard anyone, as I ran forward, holding the javelin high. Every muscle, every sinew, every centimetre of my concentration was aware of that javelin in my hand and where I wanted it to go. But as I released it into the air, I could hear the knowledgeable Finnish crowd gasp. They realised my throw was going to be a big one.

I watched it soar upward, then sail on the breeze, and then after what seemed an hour, descend in what seemed like slow motion to the ground. The throw was a good one, 69.14 metres.

I had thrown down the gauntlet. Would the towering Finn Tiina Lillak, for whom the crowd was rooting and who was the favourite, be able to pick it up?

Tensely, I waited for someone to overtake me, but after two rounds, then three, then four, no one came near – not Tessa, not even tall, thin, twenty-two-year-old Tiina, who had recently set the world record with a mammoth 72.40-metre throw. Tiina was six weeks younger than I but, at five foot eleven, she towered over me by six inches, and every inch of it was muscle. Those extra inches also gave her extra reach.

People think of me as the incredible hulk. They don't realise I am under five foot five, which is a bit of a disadvantage in the javelin. When people see me in the flesh they often tell me they are surprised at how small I am. Oh those muscles are there all right, but they hang on the runt of the litter. However, the one and only time I have yearned to be a towering giantess was on that nerve-racking 1983 Helsinki summer's day.

On that big first throw, I had felt my shoulder go, and realised that I would not myself be able to throw any further that day. But Tiina Lillak's throwing arm was working well. In the fifth round, as she took her throw, I held my breath.

But, no, the throw was short. I breathed a sigh of relief. With only one more round to go, the British commentators were getting ready to hang the gold medal around my neck. I could almost see it glittering on my breast. The unbelievable was about to happen. I was on the verge of becoming the world champion.

As Tiina, in her blue and white kit, strode out on to the run-up to take her last throw of the competition, I almost had to shut my eyes. She exuded determination from every pore. Lillak was thought to be the best javelin thrower in the world, and she was a Finn throwing for the highest honour in the world in Finland. The eyes of the crowd were glued to her, willing her to win.

Tiina stood stock still for one intense moment, all five foot eleven inches of her concentrating on where she wanted the javelin to go. Then she threw.

I watched as the javelin sailed high and wide. The crowd roared. Her throw was longer than mine, nearly 71 metres. She had snatched the gold medal. I would have to be content with silver. The crowd were on their feet. Tiina began to run a lap of the stadium, a victory lap. The Finnish crowd stayed on their feet to applaud.

Her achievement was tremendous. It had so nearly been mine. I could not help myself, I cried. I rushed to the edge of the stadium where Mum was sitting in the front row and cried my disappointment into her arms. She ruffled my hair. The television cameras saw.

148

'If the wind hadn't changed,' Sebastian Coe told a TV reporter, 'Fatima would be world champion.' Possibly he noticed that the direction of the stadium flags had shifted. Possibly the wind did change. But I don't think that was what mattered. The crowd and her own determination lifted Tiina's javelin.

What the TV didn't show – and how could they? – was how I felt by the time Mum and I left the stadium. Not happy, not by a long way, but proud of myself. Oh, I had wanted gold, I don't deny that, but that world silver medal, once I stopped to think about it, was an amazing attainment. Bronze had been my best hope. Having only just managed to qualify, I had nearly won gold and had won my first silver medal in a major championship. And I had gone to the competition with my shoulder aching and a sore throat. I had a new respect for myself and I had faith that I could count on my stamina and drive.

Tessa had never been any threat to me in that competition. She finished only fourth – out of the medals. I have to admit that that in itself was cheering. And my silver medal meant I was number two in the world, just one step from the top. Although I knew that step could take years, I tried to feel delighted.

As Mum and I walked resolutely back to the hotel, we saw grown men dancing in the street with cardboard cut-outs of Tiina Lillak.

Mum always calls me a perfectionist. I tend to give myself a hard time if I do poorly, even in training. Being fit for my sport requires an awful lot of work. I train relentlessly, every day, four times a day. I train hard and at a high standard. I've run a mile in 4 minutes 35 seconds – that could get me in the international team for 1,500 metres. My 200 metres is 24.35 seconds. I can put the shot 15.41 metres. I've done these in competition.

I never think of Mum as Mum when we go to the track or to a training session. I think of her as my coach and we just get on with it. In the beginning we used to hide behind barriers when the East Germans were training to pick up a few pointers they didn't want to give away. Mum was feeling her way intuitively in coaching while the opposition had its own sports scientists who knew how to harness the physics of the sport. Mum would talk to the Russians or Bulgarians or whomever – Todorova's coach was a good source of information – to get their views on training methods so that we could introduce them into my programme.

Not everybody was intentionally helpful, but we could learn a lot using Mum's ingenuity. Jotting down the dates on which a top thrower competed and noting how well she did, Mum was able to figure out how often one needed to compete in order to get and stay at the top. It was hit and miss for us at first, now we know better what we are doing.

I have a lot of respect for the East Europeans because I don't believe they compete under quite the ideal conditions that everybody thinks. They do have that tremendous back-up, but they miss having freedom. You can see it in their faces sometimes. And they don't get the perks and pleasures that we do. From the look of it, sometimes they don't even get nice things to eat. You should see them in the athletes' dining room at competitions, piling gâteau on top of their steaks lest it is all gone by the time they get to the second course.

You have to give them credit for the amount of work they put in, for their seriousness and achievement. In fact, it was over her attitude to a great Eastern European athlete that I lost a lot of respect for Tessa. The incident to which I am referring happened well before Helsinki, even before Athens.

Way back in 1981 I went as Tessa's back-up to the Europa Cup in Zagreb, Yugoslavia. Neither Tessa nor I, who as a reserve didn't even throw, made Zagreb remember us that day of 15 August, but the friendly Bulgarian Antoanetta Todorova, who had welcomed me in Poland, shattered the world record by more than a metre with a whacking 71.88-metre throw.

Naturally, after Tessa's defeat that day in Zagreb, I was comforting her, Brit to Brit. It was understandable that she was disappointed, but she never once acknowledged Todorova's fine performance. Instead, she tried to pass it off as a fluke, saying that Todorova would never do it again in her life.

It was outrageous. We had just seen someone throw well over

70 metres for what we regarded as the first time. We had heard of the Russian Tatyana Biryulina breaking 70 metres in Moscow the year before, but that was in Moscow. No one ever saw any film of that or saw her throw that distance again. So we had our doubts. But in Zagreb I was there and saw what Todorova could do with my own eyes, as did Tessa and the best throwers in Europe. And what we saw was awesome. Todorova was technically so astute and so consistent, and so pleasant a young woman, not big-headed or stand-offish, that one had to regard her with the utmost respect. Mum and I had had a meal with her and her coach when I won the European junior title.

Todorova was much younger than Tessa, even three months younger than me. No one knew then that her career would be retarded by injury and cut short by the death of her coach, who was like a father to her. He died of cancer. If not for that, I am sure that today Antoanetta Todorova would be my respected rival today, right up there with me and that talented East German Petra Felke.

What disillusioned me about Tessa happened in Zagreb after the competition. That evening in the hostel, the athletes assembled in the canteen to watch the highlights of the competition on the video. It was an informal occasion, with us lounging in our tracksuits. All the athletes were there, East and West. They showed Todorova's world record quite a few times, paying her the massive tribute she deserved. It was the only world record of that Europa Cup, a piece of history. She was the first woman anyone had ever seen throw 70 metres in a major competition. The only person who wasn't respectful of this achievement was Tessa. She was not very gracious in defeat. 'That wasn't a woman I was competing against today,' she said in a voice that quite a few people could hear. 'That was a chemical man.'

Todorova had never failed a drug test. She had no more muscles than Tessa did then or I have now. Antoanetta Todorova wasn't beautiful but she wasn't ugly either, and even if she were, the fact was that she was sitting in the room with us, watching the film, and Tessa knew it. Perhaps that is why she said in a louder voice, 'That's no woman, that's a man.'

151

Todorova's face went red as a beetroot. I felt embarrassed for her and ashamed to be with Tessa.

'She's sitting there, Tessa. Don't show yourself up.'

At that, Tessa shut up.

No one accomplishes anything in sport without believing in herself and without getting a lot of help.

In Helsinki I began to believe in myself more firmly and to believe in the possibility of my most ambitious dream, and I certainly do now – except on those few mornings when, like everyone else in the world, I don't. Fortunately, on those days my coach brings me a cup of tea and urges me patiently to get up and go training. If I don't, she gets less patient and more outspoken. You have to coach the mind as well as the body. She has done that from the start.

Last winter, when no one discovered for four months that a bone in my heel was out of place, the injury became so painful that I could hardly walk on it and certainly couldn't run. The treatment I was getting on my back and hamstring – cortisone, tissue manipulation – would have worked if that tiny bone had not been a fraction out of position. Understandably the foot was ignored until throwing commenced as part of my winter training in March.

Mum is my only coach but we get ideas from specialists regarding weights, bounding, running and so forth. My osteopath is Terry Moule, whom I see regularly and who is also a nutritionist. Seb Coe recommended Terry Moule, who sees a lot of British athletes and who designed the diet which makes it possible for me to build muscle. I have been going to Terry since November 1980. Willie Banks, the triple jumper, has given me good training tips. The weightlifter Geoff Capes has too. Don Quarrie has given me helpful advice on sprints, as has Linford Christie's crash coach. Sometimes I train with Verona Elder. Both she and her husband have been good to me.

I do my weight training with a partner. For years, Mick, who is a docker, and I trained in an unheated garage about five minutes from home. It was so cold in the winter, that each time I put another weight on the bar, I felt I was picking up a chunk of ice.

I still do my weight training in Mick's garage, but as Mick can no longer get off work, Mum helps me out now.

Victory is sweet, they say. Like expensive chocolate. The truth is that the taste of victory – imminent victory – was in my case strawberry-flavoured Complan. I had been drinking four, five, even six glasses of it every day for three years. But hard graft and a good foundation aren't enough to become a winner. It takes magic. The real alchemy of Helsinki, the magic, was that it transformed me into a world-reckoned winner.

Just a week after the Worlds, I transmuted silver into gold at the 1983 Europa Cup. This time I was no one's back-up. I was the British number one. But I was Antoanetta Todorova's heiress. She had won it the previous time; this year it belonged to me. Mine was the first gold medal ever won by a British woman in a European throwing event. I knew I was on my way.

Three or four days later I had my tonsils out. I wouldn't miss them. That was a small problem, but even the big ones, I sensed, would no longer deflect me. Not my grief which was always there. Not my shoulder or back pain. Not even an operation for fibroids two months before I threw 69 metres at the Talbot Games.

Until that summer of 1983, though, Tessa had always been there, a bit ahead. In a way Tessa had been a help, an inspiration. She was five years older than me, five years further along the way, and always up there, the British number one, something to aim at.

I always knew that one day I would take on the mantle. Perhaps Tessa knew it too. Maybe that's why she has said some snide and utterly untrue things about me and Mum. Funny isn't it that *after* I had been the victim of a pro-Tessa, hate-mail campaign of anonymous letters – which I reported to the police – she then decided that she too had been the victim of such a campaign.

I have more sympathy for Tessa on the issue of anabolic steroids – which she has been suspected of taking, as have I. Tessa denies vociferously that she has ever taken these or any other illegal drugs, as I do. I have never taken such drugs and I never will. In Britain we have the best scrutiny of athletes in the world. It would be impossible to cheat if you wanted to. I don't want to. And it is perfectly right that people who do cheat get caught.

They are ruining our sport. Anna Verouli, the Greek girl, who was a one-year wonder, going from eleventh place in the World Student Games to gold in the European Javelin Championship in that short time, tested positive for anabolic steroids at the Los Angeles Olympics. Many people think Anna must have had the benefit of those muscle-building drugs when she won in Athens. On a personal level, she was all right so far as I knew her. Professionally, though, she was a cheat, and in LA she got her come-uppance.

If it were possible I would be friends with Tessa — and it was nearly possible. Mum was a fan of Tessa's early on, and was team manager when Tessa broke the British record in West Germany. Mum was delighted. But later, when she felt me creeping up the ranks, Tessa began to throw stones.

Apart from everything else, the distance between our respective homes is a barrier. Tessa lives in Leeds and I live in Essex. But since it is very difficult when you reach a certain standard to keep pushing yourself further, it would be nice occasionally to train alongside Tessa, as I sometimes do with Verona.

Perhaps our rivalry is just in the nature of things. Maybe neither of us is to blame. All those years, Tessa was always there, I was right behind her. I experienced her as a barrier to overcome. But to her, I must have been a nuisance breathing down her neck.

And Los Angeles was looming.

That winter, though, my training was hampered somewhat by severe pelvic pain. The doctor diagnosed fibroids, growths on my womb, which had to be cauterised. When that didn't quite work, I went back for a second cauterisation, and I was recovering nicely. Then, just two weeks before I had to depart for the Games I had to go in and have the fibroids cauterised for a third time. I felt weak and a little wobbly. The doctor told my mother it was not advisable for me to compete in the 1984 Olympics. It was too soon.

Mum said it would have to be my decision. I wanted desperately to go to Los Angeles. So I decided to disobey doctor's orders. Even if it didn't help my fibroid condition one bit, I knew I had to have a go. I tried to keep secret the fact that I had had a third fibroid operation so near to the Games. But the *News of the World* printed the story.

In hindsight, perhaps by going to LA, I did the wrong thing. I did have a lot of trouble afterwards, until January of the next year. It has never been reported in the press.

But because of Helsinki, I was down as the favourite, according to the British press. They said I had a good chance at winning gold. Also I was throwing better than Tessa Sanderson. No one had any hope for Tessa. The press kept ignoring her and interviewing me. Tessa, I hear, was not pleased, especially when it was reported that her Olympic prospects were nil or poor. The British press, who had reported her career so vociferously, felt it was ending. Now the press had their eyes on me. They felt I was on my way up, and she on her way down. Tessa was twenty-eight, five years older than I was, but her age was no disadvantage. Javelin throwers mature like wine.

My only edge was that I was getting better with every throw. After those thorny European Championships in Athens, I replaced her as the British number one in the javelin rankings, a spot she had held unchallenged for a decade. I knew I had a reasonable chance at a medal, even in my weakened state, and knew I would never forgive myself if I put the Olympics on hold for another four years.

Tessa was going, despite the fact that the press had told her to her face that she was past it. This was unfair. Even I felt sympathy. Because at the height of her career, in 1980, Tessa had failed to qualify for the Moscow Olympic final, now some of the tabloid toughies suggested that it was a foregone conclusion that Tessa would fail in LA. But I knew she had been training hard and she had a lot of bulk on her, a lot of muscle. She was two inches taller than me and on the eve of the Olympic final, for which both of us had qualified, she outweighed me by a stone. I had to give her credit. She was all muscle.

LA, the smog capital of the world, was choking, nearly as hot as Athens and more humid. Physically the weather was annoying. Technically, it was fascinating. Because humidity expands the javelin and gives it lift, that high humidity could, particularly if there was a little wind, make for record-shattering throws.

But the final was not until early evening, when the stadium had cooled off. Not a lot mind you, just a bit. There was a hint of a breeze. I knew that my throw would have to be high and dead centre to float the javelin on so tepid a current of air.

This time, to my amazement, it was Tessa who threw down the gauntlet on her first throw. Running fast, holding the javelin high, she hurled it hard. I could see at once from the angle of release that it would be a long throw. But would it be long enough to do any damage?

The javelin plopped to the ground at the 69.56-metre mark. That was impressive. I was excited for Tessa, honestly. I also felt a twinge of sadness. Then I remembered, I had five more rounds to beat it. So did the world champion Tiina Lillak, who now held her second world javelin record, and who was at the time, without a doubt, the best thrower of the three of us. But Tiina, who was walking gingerly, was suffering from a stress fracture of her foot which was disastrous for her run-up.

In the second round, I inched closer with 65.42 metres, still no danger at all.

Then Tiina gritted her teeth and let go a knockout throw, which landed just short of victory, at 69.00. One more and she might have made it, but Tiina had made her ankle hurt and took no more throws.

I kept trying. On my fifth throw I moved into bronze medal position with 67.14. I had felt weak throughout the competition. There was only one more throw; I knew I had to make it count. To be perfectly honest, I didn't mind losing to Tiina, a great champion in her prime, but I hated the idea of losing at this late date to Tessa Sanderson.

The floodlights went on in the stadium. The crowd was as tense as I was, even though it was an American crowd, and there was no American in the running. Holding the javelin aloft, I ran with it, and let it go. But at the moment I let go, I knew it was not the throw I wanted. It would fall short.

Tessa was the Olympic champion. Not only had she set an Olympic record, she had become the first British woman and the first black woman of any nationality to win an Olympic throwing event. A disappointed Tiina had won silver. I had to make do with bronze. There was no way I could feel delighted. I could not help myself. I cried again with the cameras watching. But that was in the heat of the moment. Pulling myself together I went over and congratulated Tessa. Her achievement was tremendous, and my own was not dreadfully bad. I was now an Olympian. My bronze medal would always be there in the Olympic annals.

Later, as Tessa, Tiina and I stood together on the victory podium, medals hanging like necklaces around our necks, the sound of our national anthem being played and seeing Tessa crying touched me. I just had to reach up and give her a little tweak on the cheek. Touching her cheek like that, spontaneously, was a gesture of affection. An accolade. We were both Brits, we had known each other a long time. Her joy, her big smile, brighter than a toothpaste advert, was contagious. At that moment I felt happy for her. But even as Tessa cried for joy, Tiina's disappointment brimmed over, and tears streamed down her cheek.

That reminded me of my own disappointment. I had wanted gold. If I hadn't had to have that third operation so close to the Olympics who knows what would have happened? Similarly, if Tiina hadn't been injured, and if the East Germans hadn't boycotted the Olympics – if Petra Felke had been there – what would the outcome have been? But sport is about who is best on the day. It had been Tessa's day. I would just have to wait for another chance, four years, until the next Olympics in Seoul in 1988.

Four years seemed a long time to me, but I had no idea that such a lot could happen in the interim. In 1985, when Tessa and I competed for the first time after the Olympics, at Gateshead, I easily beat her by almost 15 feet with a throw of 225 feet 10 inches (68.84 metres). But after the javelin competition verbal darts began to fly. We had been friendly rivals; now there was a lot of nastiness.

There were the ups and downs of competition after that, mostly ups. Then something entirely unpredictable, something terrible happened in December.

13

Heaven and Hell

Four days before Christmas my fifteen-year-old brother Gregg got out of bed and his legs buckled under him. Unable to stand up, he lay sprawled on the floor, helpless. Mum drove him to Casualty within the hour and our GP phoned to say she was on her way. But by the time they got to Oldchurch Hospital in Romford Gregg's hands were useless too. Only the day before, Gregg had been a strong, apparently healthy young lad, running around doing this and that. Now he was completely paralysed. The suddenness of what had happened was terrifying. The doctor said he had Guillain-Barré syndrome, which can be fatal. Mum and Dad were badly shaken and worried, as were my other brother Kirk and I. Gregg himself, who didn't know if he would ever have any strength in his limbs again, or even if he would live, was remarkably self-contained. I have never seen anyone be so quietly brave.

About seventy people in Britain come down with the rare Guillain-Barré syndrome every year, but no one knows what causes it to pick those particular people, and once the disease becomes full-blown, there is no known medication. You have to wait the virus out, sometimes for years.

Joseph Heller, who wrote that famous novel *Catch 22*, got Guillain-Barré when he was in his sixties and was hospitalised for six months. He left in a wheelchair and some years later is still not completely right.

If the doctors diagnose GB in the first three days, they can give the patient a complete plasma change, but that didn't happen in my brother's case.

For four months Gregg lay in bed in Oldchurch Hospital, a

158

horribly run-down-looking, depressing place. In fact, it looks like a nineteenth-century workhouse and inspired little confidence. But appearances can be deceptive – the nursing staff are superb. We went to see Gregg in hospital twice a day. He was amazing. As we sat around his hospital bed, he told *us* not to worry and tried to hide the anxious look in his blue eyes.

We have BUPA insurance and wanted to transfer him to a cheerier hospital immediately, but we had to wait those four months until he was out of danger, because private hospitals like Hartswood-Essex in Brentwood where he spent six more weeks, only do general nursing. They don't offer the specialised nursing skills you get in a National Health hospital.

At Oldchurch the attitude was: just give the disease time and the paralysis would slowly lift. Eventually, they did send a physiotherapist in to see Gregg three times a week to help him re-educate his limbs and stimulate the nerve pathways. But my instinct was that it wasn't often enough. Of course, Oldchurch, being a National Health hospital, was under financial strain. There were too few physiotherapists available to treat too many patients. But I had only one brother in hospital.

Against the doctors' better judgement, I massaged Gregg's limbs two or three times a week. More would have been too tiring for him. Having had so much manipulation for my own injuries, I felt I knew what I was doing, even though I realised all too well I was not medically trained. I would raise Gregg's legs for him to help his tummy muscles. I also gave him some exercises he could do in his hospital bed, and did some of them with him. He could reach up to the iron bars at the head of the bed and stretch a little. He did it as often as he possibly could. I would leave him a sponge ball to squeeze and later, when he was able, a squash ball. I felt such joy the first time he had strength enough to pick up a small cube. I could see he felt immense relief. The exercises were very important. Otherwise, lying in that bed like a vegetable, he would find that when he did walk again, his muscles would have atrophied and recovery would be harder than ever. The doctor and the hospital physio did not ban my ministrations. They merely said it wouldn't help him. I persisted anyway.

159

Visiting Gregg was taking a lot of time from my winter training at a crucial period. Unlike bears, athletes don't hibernate during the winter. We put in plenty of hard graft, laying down the foundation that will build into the summer's success. Three hard sessions a day, six days a week. As Tessa's coach, Wilf Paish, a dapper, moustached chap, who also coaches the top British male javelin thrower Mick Hill, says, a javelin thrower really has to be 'the complete athlete'.

I no longer run repetition 50s, dragging behind me a tyre tied by a rope to my waist, but I weight-train five times a week. And I like to get in a four-mile endurance run at quite a good speed every Monday or Wednesday, and sprint, bound and throw a medicine ball 150 times a week.

Mum has to be there when we do our technical work. For example, it is she who throws me the four-kilo medicine ball over and over again at exactly the right angle, so that I can catch it using the muscles of my arms, back and legs in a way that is similar to throwing a javelin. When I am doing my squats and jumps, the floor of the gym vibrates with activity.

The Commonwealth Games and the European Championships were coming that following summer. I wanted to win either or both badly, and I knew that going to and from the hospital to see Gregg was cutting into my training. But the Whitbread family had always given emotional support to me. For the first time I could be an emotional support to them. My father, who is a sensitive soul, a lovable softy, was very upset. My mother needed a shoulder too. Kirk was as shocked as the rest of us. I felt I had to try to be strong for them. I decided my brother was more important than a gold medal.

And poor Gregg, he was undergoing the agony of not knowing when or if he would ever walk again. He was worried too because he was missing his O levels. And he was worried that I was losing time from my training. 'That's not a problem,' I said, promising I would win the Commonwealth Games gold medal for him.

The months which followed were very traumatic for every member of the family. Visiting that dreary hospital, giving him the massage and exercises, later bathing him and urging him to use the wheelchair and then the walking frame. I had always loved him. Now, as I saw how he bore his unfortunate illness, I gained a new respect for him.

He had fought to get well, insisting on exercising even a little finger as soon as he possibly could. In only a few months he was leading almost a normal life. Gregg made a faster advance than many people. Usually, recovery is in two years, or never. We know now that our instinct to speed his recovery with massage and exercise was correct.

In May 1986 Gregg and his wheelchair accompanied Mum, Dad, Kirk and me to Cyprus for spring training. The warm weather and the change in environment were a boon to us all.

In the summer, he went in his wheelchair to take his O levels. His handwriting, which never had been a calligrapher's dream, had deteriorated badly and Mum got a certificate from a doctor explaining to the examiners. Despite having been so ill, and still not fully recovered, he took and passed four O levels. I was so proud of him.

At the end of July, I flew to Edinburgh for the Commonwealth Games where there was a lot of aggro because of Zola Budd. Although the Games were supposed to bring the Commonwealth together, this time they were tearing it apart. The Games were turning into an international catastrophe.

For me personally, those Games were a catastrophe too. The Commonwealth standard is not that high. When I saw my javelin traverse a respectable 224 feet 10 inches (68.54 metres) before plopping on to the waterlogged turf at the Meadowbank Stadium, a throw that put me in the lead, I felt I had the competition wrapped up. But Tessa propelled her javelin more than four feet further, 229 feet (69.80 metres) to victory.

As a family we had had a lot to cope with. I wanted that gold medal for Gregg. Silver wouldn't do. When Tessa won and I didn't, I couldn't help myself. I cried. Again, the world saw me in tears, and Tessa celebrating.

As I sat sobbing into the plaid blanket I had brought to dry off from the rain, the hurdler Wendy Jeal, who is one of my closest friends, rushed over to comfort me. Mum hurried over too. When

I pulled myself together, we walked off arm in arm. It is hard to believe that as low as I felt, I had the presence of mind to tell the man from the *Daily Telegraph*, 'Some day someone up there will look down on me.' I couldn't have believed it very much at that moment. But it was a prediction that would very soon come true.

I know now that in the build-up period to the Commonwealth Games I made two mistakes. They were entirely my own fault, and I don't think I'll make those particular mistakes again. (No doubt I will make others.) My first stupid mistake was promising to win the gold medal for Gregg. He had not asked me to, I offered. I don't like to break promises, so the pressure I had put on myself to win was tremendous. My second error was that I had had too little preliminary competition, which I now know I need, to have a properly sharp edge on the big day. At the last minute I had decided not to go as planned to an invitational meeting in Europe. It seemed too far because as a family we had so much on. What I needed, I realise all too clearly in hindsight, was a zappy little competition somewhere nearer to home. But no one was likely to be able to lay one on at such short notice. And anyway, it didn't occur to me to ask. So I felt like a pressure cooker when I walked out on to the field in Edinburgh, when I should have been a razor-sharp carving knife.

Losing at the Commonwealth Games hurt. Pride goeth before a fall, the saying goes. After that embarrassing defeat, my pride lay in a bruised heap. I felt guilty too. I had let Gregg down. Mum said that that was nonsense. Gregg said that it was nonsense too. I had done my best. You can't, he said, do any more. Compared to the difficulties in our lives which had preceded it, of course, defeat in the Commonwealth was paltry.

The fact was, things had been going wrong for a long time in my life. Disaster seemed to be following upon disaster. I had no luck. Even more horrifying, those near and dear to me seemed to have no luck either. Was my misfortune rubbing off on them?

Mum said that I wasn't causing any bad luck and that thinking it was more nonsense, the javelin would come right. Every dog has its day, she told me. She said that she was speaking not only as a mother but as a coach, the voice of authority. 'On both counts,' she said, 'you had better listen, Fatima. And while you are at it, stop that whinging and whining.'

I did stop whinging, and I did stop whining, but I couldn't help wondering. Was heartbreak on and off the competition field going to be my lot in life forever?

Four weeks after the Commonwealth disaster, without much hope, I flew to West Germany with Mum for the most prestigious javelin event of the year, the European Championships.

Looking out of the window of our Stuttgart hotel room at six a.m. on the morning of 28 August 1986, I saw that the day was not promising. It was cold, dull and damp, classic British summer weather, which, I now realised, was probably also classically German. Six a.m. was early for me, earlier than I needed to get up, but I just couldn't sleep.

Mum made us each a cup of tea and we munched a few plain biscuits she had brought from home. Saying little, we got up slowly, as there was plenty of time before I had to go to the stadium for the qualifying round, an unglamorous but crucial stage of every athletic competition. Only if I qualified this morning would I compete in the final tomorrow.

The press were cracking the lids off soft-boiled eggs and lathering *Brot* with butter on that grey summer morning when Mum and I left for Neckar Stadium. The stadium was nearly empty, the stands entirely deserted. There is no energy boost from an empty stadium, whereas a crowded one is electric. Only the prospective competitors, their coaches and advisers, and a handful of school children were at Neckar that grey summer's morning.

Tessa was not in Stuttgart. The story was that she was injured but *The Times* report said: 'There is more than a suspicion that her advisers had prevailed upon Tessa not to risk her public image after Edinburgh by coming here and competing against sterner opposition.'

Burly Ruth Fuchs, the legendary East German thrower of the preceding generation was at Neckar, though supporting East Germany's current champion Petra Felke, a lanky, pretty blonde who

163

held the world record. Petra was the favourite to win the championship.

I was to throw in the first pool of qualifiers. But Petra was throwing with the second pool. She would have no trouble qualifying, nor, did I expect, would I. To qualify, we each had to throw a distance of 62 metres, a fair distance for some but not for me. It was much less even than my losing throw at the Commonwealth Games, the one which had only been good enough for a silver medal. Although I had three throws in which to qualify, I hoped to do it on the first throw so that we could get out of this wintry summer weather and back to the warmth of the hotel. Then I could lounge around and rest up for the real job of the weekend, the final.

It was an almost windless morning. The West German thrower Ingrid Thyssen was just before me and threw 65 metres looking very comfortable. I thought if she can do that distance, I shouldn't have any problems.

Picking up the javelin for my first throw, holding it high, I focussed only on where that javelin was going, not why, I began my run-up, eleven strides, fast, faster, even faster. Every instant of my run-up flowed, and at the power-packed moment of release, everything felt just right. I let the javelin, which was now pointing skywards, explode like a missile from the gantry of my hand.

As the javelin soared away, I thought that's my job over for the day. It was going to be a long throw. I watched the javelin soar higher, slicing cleanly through the bread-thick air. Looking across the field at the yellow line marked at 65 metres, I waited for the javelin to land, but it was still sailing on that damp air. It was going to be a *very* long throw.

The judges scampered further out on the field. I bit my lower lip, and after what seemed a century but was only seconds, my beautiful javelin began its swift descent, landing softly on the turf. The judges put the marker down at 77.44 metres, which was 254 feet. I had broken the world record. And my new world record beat the previous best, Petra Felke's record, by a gargantuan 2 metres 4 centimetres. In other words, I had not chipped the record, I had smashed it, by 6 feet $8\frac{1}{2}$ inches.

164

Ecstatic, I could hardly believe it. Not only had I broken the world record, but I had shattered a psychological barrier in my sport. I was now the only woman in the world who had ever hurled a javelin 250 feet, which many people had thought no woman would ever be able to do. I gave a whoop of victory and smiled and smiled and smiled. By now, my tears were almost as well known to Britons as Olga Korbut's were to the world. But, at last, on this dreary morning, 28 August 1986, I had reason to smile. At 8.18 in the morning, British summer time, in an empty stadium in Stuttgart, I had hurled my javelin further than any woman ever had before. These things happen when you least expect them.

Mum signalled to me to grab my kit so that we could get away, but then we both realised that was no longer possible. Because I had set a world record, I had to undergo a drug test. Instead of hurrying back to the hotel we had to wait about an hour for the testers to get to the stadium. All world records require that test.

By the time the staff had arrived with their beakers and, under their scrutiny, I had provided a urine sample, word of my achievement had reached the media. They were everywhere, full of goodwill, but bombarding me in a dozen languages. Was I happy to have set a record? Was it a surprise? And, *Fräulein*, do you like Stuttgart? You know the sort of thing. The answers were obvious. But it was their job to ask those questions, and I replied to all of them. It is all part of the service! The athletics correspondents, the specialists, asked a few more astute questions. I tried to give them good answers.

Later, Petra Felke, who was the second highest qualifier, told the man from *The Times* that she had been less surprised than I was at my throw. 'I always thought that Fatima had got one or two really great throws in her,' she said, 'But I still think I can win with 74 metres.'

We didn't actually see Petra to talk to until the next day, but Mum had also told the journalists that Petra, who had been as consistent a thrower as I was, but at a slightly higher standard, was still the favourite. What Mum didn't say was that I had wrenched my arm in the qualifying round.

As soon as we could, Mum and I hurried back to the hotel, where we ate our takeaway lunch. I spent the rest of the day in bed lazing about and watching German TV. Often my world record was shown – it was in the introduction and at the end of each sports programme. In between, there was me winking happily and blowing a kiss, which, evidently, is what I did at the height of my jubilation.

Our evening meal, which we also had in our room, was as unexciting as lunch – rolls stuffed with ham and cheese, biscuits and a mug of hot chocolate. This was all part of the strategy for staying calm for tomorrow's final. That was the only problem now. There was no worry about the drug test because I never took any illegal drugs. And, as I expected, in due course, my world record was ratified.

But my wrenched shoulder was worrying. It still hurt. With an injured throwing arm, how could I even hope for a medal, let alone victory? Was the price of my world record going to be the gold medal? Was gold in major competition going to elude me yet again?

Just such a catastrophe had happened over twenty years ago to the greatest javelin thrower of her time, the Russian Yelena Gorchakova. In the qualifying round of the 1964 Olympics, Yelena set a then world record of 62.40 metres, but in the final she couldn't manage any more than 57.06 metres. She didn't get a medal. Gold went to a Romanian, but Yelena Gorchakova's world record remained unbroken for fully eight years – the longest time any javelin record has stood. Every serious javelin thrower knows Yelena's story.

I went to bed that night with more than an aching shoulder. I didn't sleep well. The next morning I stayed in bed until 11 a.m., and had nothing but a cup of tea until Mum and I walked over to a nearby restaurant, and although we were in Germany, I had a big plate of spaghetti bolognese for lunch. I couldn't eat all of it. My stomach was in knots. The day was as grey as my prospects.

Back at the hotel I had a fitful little nap. At five p.m. we left for the stadium. Maurie, our driver, who is Australian, passed as a TV crew technician to get us close to the entrance.

166

The warming-up area was very crowded. As I strode on to the field, Petra Felke, a gracious opponent, rushed forward to congratulate me on my world record. Hugging me, she said, 'To me it was not a surprise. I believed in your ability.' Petra's coach Helmann congratulated me too.

The bell sounded for the end of the warm-up. As the other finalists made their way to the reporting room, I had a couple more throws, concentrating in turn on the positioning of my hips, shoulder and arm. Mum was a bundle of tension. She was quivering so much she could barely talk. She told me after the competition that she had gone straight to the toilet and had a little cry and a pray before making her way to her seat behind the javelin run-up.

As the competition began, the rain was hammering down. Myself, I was used to throwing in the rain, but I wondered how Petra would cope. Petra took an early lead, and my arm hurt. After each throw, I held my shoulder to keep it warm. Mum who was watching on the huge stadium television, which shows the action larger than life, realised that it must be throbbing. For rounds one, two and three, Petra continued to lead the competition. I tried to keep the growing sense of hopelessness off my face.

Between throws, I bundled into my tracksuit and huddled under the small, roofed, open-walled shelter, rather like a bus stop shelter, which they had there. I watched as between rounds the West Germans brought on a big machine to sponge the water off the runway.

The throws in the rain were not impressive, but Petra's were more impressive than mine. My throws, though, were, I realised with some comfort, going further with each round. I was beginning to click. The rain let up, and on the fourth round I took the lead by a few centimetres, with a throw of 72.68. Petra, who was throwing ahead of me, could do no better than 72 on her fourth, fifth, and sixth throws.

Even with my shoulder aching, I had squeaked to victory. There was no need to take my last throw.

But the story was not over yet. I did not really want to win the European Championship by a hair. I didn't want anyone any-where – including myself – to think my victory was an accident, a fluke. I was entitled to one more throw at this competition, and as I had nothing to lose and everything to gain, I decided to take it. If it was a good throw, it would underline my superiority, giving my future opponents a little lesson, giving me a decisive win, not a near one. And it would show me just how well I can perform when I'm relaxed even if I am hampered by injury.

With no further need to protect my arm for an answering throw, I stood on the runway and let rip. Yes, yes, I was right, it was going to go far. My sixth throw, which I had been under no obligation to take, landed at 76.32 metres, making it the second furthest throw in the world – bettered only by the new world record I had set the day before. I had not only won, I had won well.

I had done it. In the face of javelin history, I had done it. I had won.

All the years of training had finally come to something. What a weekend I was having. I went on my lap of honour, with the photographers running backwards in front of me, trying to get their shots. After the victory lap, I would willingly pause for them, but not during my victory lap. Exultant, throwing kisses to the cheering crowd, I thanked God every step of the way. Spontaneously, I wiggled my hips in happiness, a victory wiggle.

I stopped briefly to shake Wendy Jeal's hand and to hug and kiss Arne De Jong, the physio from Holland who had given me treatment. When I got to where Mum was sitting in the stands, I saw that she was smiling and crying at the same time.

Petra, ever gracious, came over and congratulated me on my second achievement of the weekend. She had arrived in Stuttgart as the world record holder and as the hot favourite for gold. She had thrown well, but she would leave with neither. I felt for her. But mostly I felt joy at my triumph. It healed a lot of wounds. Not only was I the champion of Europe, but with one fell swoop, I also claimed the British and Commonwealth records, both of which Tessa had held for twelve years. I always knew I would put it all together one day. Now I had done it.

With only one exception – and that was my own Europa Cup victory in 1983 – no British woman in history had ever succeeded in winning a major throwing event in which the best javelin throwers, the Eastern Europeans, had competed. Tessa's Olympic victory and my own Olympic bronze medal had been won in their absence. But they were here at the European Championships. And as ever, they were the ones to beat.

And now I held the world record too. I was the first Briton of either sex to hold a world record in a throwing event. What a weekend. Yes, I told the German journalists who asked me, Fräulein Whitbread was enjoying her stay in West Germany.

14

On Top of the World

This is the nightmare I woke up from dreaming three days before the World Championships. I am driving the car as carefully as I can because it is a winding road and there is a sheer drop. All of a sudden, one of the curves is too sharp, and the car veers out of control and over the top of the cliff. It is falling, falling, and I am trapped. The door won't open, or there is no door. The glass of the windscreen is as hard as lead, or is made of brick. The windows are locked, permanently sealed. I can't get out. I can't escape. The car, with me in it, is about to crash.

Waking up suddenly in my hotel room in Rome, a mass of jangling nerve endings, I told myself this dream meant only one thing: I had to make myself relax. It was a classic anxiety dream, the sort of dream I and so many other athletes have in the days before a big competition.

I went back to sleep. I might have a nightmare again tomorrow night, but at least the next night, the one before the competition, I knew I would have no bad dreams. I never have nightmares on the eve of a competition because I don't sleep much.

I had almost stayed home from these World Championships. A year after my triumph in Stuttgart, once again everything looked bleak. In Oslo on 4 July, I had defeated Petra Felke soundly, which ordinarily would have caused me to celebrate my independence from her as a rival, but for one mishap. I fell on my throwing arm, not only aggravating an injury I had sustained that winter in training, but burning the skin of my throwing arm, cracking a bone in my wrist, and hurting my back, arm and shoulder. The problem with my shoulder, neck, and throwing arm would not go away.

170

Then, on 29 July, one day before her twenty-eighth birthday, Petra gave herself an early birthday present, the world record, which had been mine. Her throw of 78.90 metres eclipsed my record by almost 1.5 metres. That news didn't help my aching shoulder one bit. Neither, it seemed, did anything else, not cortisone, nor soft tissue manipulation.

Sport can be a roller-coaster of emotion, the exhilaration of triumph soon giving way to sorrow – and then, if you work like a winner and the gods smile, to triumph again. Despite Rudyard Kipling's famous poem, it is impossible to treat 'those two imposters', triumph and disaster, just the same. Kipling was a poet but he was not a sports competitor.

Throughout August my shoulder gave me nothing but trouble. Unable to train, unable to sleep properly, I felt at twenty-six like an old lady, not an international athlete. Consulting a specialist as well as my osteopath, who was very experienced, I still found nothing to relieve my injury. I wasn't sure there was any reason for me to go to the competition. Unless I could throw 100 per cent in Rome, I didn't want to go. Who wants to go lame to the World Championships?

The World Athletics Championships began. All the British athletes went, and I was still in Britain, getting manipulation from Terry Moule. At that moment there still seemed no point in my going to Rome. Because my event wasn't till the very last day of the championships, with qualifying the day before, I could go late if there was any reason to.

Hoping my shoulder would stop hurting so much, hoping it would mend, I continued to go for treatment. To be honest, it didn't quite. I remember going with trepidation to Crawley to take part in the quiet little competition which had long been scheduled as part of my pre-Rome build-up. My worry was only because I had no confidence in my arm and shoulder.

I was surrounded by well wishers. Along with my coach Mum, there was Peter Yates, the British international, and Steve Backley, the European Junior champion, and Andy Norman, the British athletics promotions officer, whom I had known since I was fifteen and who was a friend of mine and a friend of the family, filming my efforts with a video camera so that we could sit down later and study any errors in my form.

At Crawley, I was delighted – and surprised – to throw 74.74 metres, not bad at any time, and terrific at a low-key competition. I threw well at Dartford, but my arm still hurt.

Mum, Andy and I got into the car and drove straight to Crystal Palace for a check-up from Dr Ken Kingsbury, who is a medical adviser to the Sports Council. Ken, a wise, greying, Seb Coe-sized man in his fifties, gave me another hefty cortisone injection.

Four days before the javelin competition we all accepted that I would never be perfectly fit in time for the World Championships. I decided to fly to Rome anyway. I would have no time to acclimatise to the heat and humidity, and I was worried about the shoulder which was still very painful. But it would be a bad omen to miss the World Championships. As we got on the plane at Heathrow, I could see worry in Mum's blue eyes.

As ever, I shared a hotel room with Mum not far from the stadium. Waking up at the Holiday Inn on Sunday morning, 'The Day,' with my stomach aflutter, even Mum's constant chatter couldn't keep my mind off the forthcoming competition. I had qualified for the final the day before, but only on my second throw. That hadn't made me feel any surer and I could tell by all her prattle that Mum was wound-up tighter even than I.

We had both slept badly, plagued by the buzz and bites of whirring mosquitoes most of the night. We were eager, both of us, to get out of that room. Lunch was my usual, a small portion of spaghetti bolognese. I ate it in a Rome restaurant five hours before the competition. I wouldn't have another meal before the competition. The five-hour interim, I had learned from experience, was about right.

It was a sweltering day. I spent the afternoon in bed, listening to tapes. The mosquitoes had taken the afternoon off. But there were butterflies in my stomach. Then it was time to go. The hotel was about two miles from the stadium. ITV had laid on a taxi. Our driver burrowed through the crazy Roman traffic, and dropped us at the warm-up area. There were no live spectators in the stadium where the athletes warmed up, but we were watched by statues of the gods of Rome.

As I walked on to the field in my GB track suit, which despite the heat and the killing humidity I wore out of habit and pride and to keep my muscles fluid, I did not feel confident. I had no reason to feel confident. But I felt better than I had expected to.

Dozens of track and field athletes were stretching, twisting, jogging on the spot and taking little practice throws that would whizz past your ear. It was actually dangerous. The chaos of the field was potentially as lethal as driving on the streets of Rome, where, it was my impression, drivers shut their eyes and stepped on the accelerator.

I began to jog around the stadium. Petra arrived with her coach Helmann. In her blue vest and white shorts, her hair a shade blonder than it had been last year, Petra looked very sure of herself. At nearly five foot seven inches, she carried her musculature well. Her knee was swathed in the bandages that were almost her trademark, but she was walking well.

As I jogged round, I stopped and walked over to her. It was the first time I had seen her since she had set the new world record, the one that had been mine, and I congratulated her. Petra, gracious in victory as in defeat, said that she knew the record would not stand still. 'I have not heard the last from you on this issue,' she said in her broken English, adding gently, 'And think you have not heard all from me.' We shook hands, and I carried on jogging.

I liked her so much. We could spur each other on, to see how far a woman could throw. Like me, Petra would do everything she could to raise the standard of achievement. She was a worthy opponent, and I felt, a friend. If not for the geographical distance between us and the political distance between our two countries, we might even be closer friends.

Yesterday Petra had qualified easily, whilst I, suffering from my hurt shoulder, trying not to damage it further before the final, had only qualified on my second throw. And Petra had qualified with the furthest throw. Mine was second furthest. That was worrying.

Tessa was warming up with her coach, Wilf Paish. She was much, much thinner than she had been in Los Angeles, too thin, I

173

felt, to be much of a threat at this level of competition. For the past year Tessa had let it be known she was training for her former event, the heptathlon, which required less weight. She had her eye on TV appearance money too. When her hopes in the heptathlon seemed unrealisable, Tessa switched back to the javelin.

Sixteen days ago, when my arm hurt so much that I could only throw a pitiful distance, I had gone like a lamb to the slaughter to Crystal Palace where Tessa, ranked only fifteenth in the world and supposedly at the top of her current form, beat me at the Dairy Crest Games. It was my first defeat in a year, and she had won with just 64 metres, a paltry throw.

I went to that meeting because I had to. If I had not gone there, then later gone to Rome there would have been snide remarks that I had let the organiser down, that I had snubbed TV and was so big for my breeches that I had failed to show up even to earn the guaranteed £10,000 in subvention money, money which goes into a trust fund until I retire from competition. The payments are set by the sport's governing body. Sebastian Coe and Steve Cram received £15,000 per televised British meeting. In 1988, the payments were reduced, mine to £5,000.

At Crystal Palace I had tried to do my best so long as it did not hurt my arm. That was one defeat which in no way shook my confidence.

Tessa's best throw of the year had been only 66.10 metres, well down on her pre-Los Angeles best, and fully 12 metres below the world record. But you never quite knew about Tessa. Although she was an unlikely winner, she just might make the medals.

Many people had written me off after Crystal Palace, saying I had gone off the boil. But I knew in my heart I was now a better thrower than Tessa was, and the rankings proved it. If we both won medals for Britain, that would be superb. I wished her well.

Now, I did a little throwing, and then I went down to the reporting area. Soon, I and the other athletes were shepherded into the tunnel to await the moment when we would be called into the Coliseum to compete. It was damp in the tunnel. Because of some delay, we were kept there for much too long, and some of the athletes bounced a ball against the metal walls to keep limber. The sound of the ball ricocheting against the wall began to give me a headache.

At last we were allowed to go into the stadium. I grabbed a spot under an umbrella out of the sun and sat down to wait for my turn to throw. I took a deep breath. The final was about to begin.

Petra and Tessa were as keyed up as I was. Beate Peters looked raring to go too. Beate, a lively, dark-haired West German, had been coming up steadily all season. It would not surprise me at all if today she was right up there with the leaders.

Looking up at the stands crowded with people and beyond to the hills of Rome, I wondered what I was doing here. There was little chance I could make a respectable throw in my condition. Why had I come to disgrace myself?

Stop it, I told myself, these are not the thoughts of a world champion. It was time now to commit myself to the competition, to put aside my doubts. Winning was what being in Rome was all about. And considering that my arm hurt and my stomach was restless, I felt remarkably good, even in that sapping heat. Staying away from Rome till the last minute had been a clever accident. No athlete who didn't live with it could fully acclimatise in a few days or even in a few weeks to the heat and humidity. At least I had given the Italian September less chance than it might have had to wear me down.

I had been a tangle of nerves when it looked as if I would not be fit for the championships. Now, in comparison, I was calm. I took my first throw. To my dismay, I managed only a pathetic 61.80 metres.

Then I watched with trepidation and some admiration as Petra bounded up the runway, and gave her javelin a mighty throw that soared just over 70 metres.

Petra increased her lead by 2 metres to 71.76 on her next throw. But although I improved dramatically, fully 7 metres, to 69.02, she still held the lead.

On my third throw I inched up even closer to 71.34. I was only half a metre behind her now, but my arm hurt. I was nearly there. I was in silver medal position, Beate Peters in bronze. Oh God, I thought, have pity on me now — and on my aching shoulder. It had been years since I had been so unlikely to do well in a competition. Although, because of my injury, my throwing so far didn't show it, I was giving it my all. This competition was like pulling tusks from an elephant.

As I waited for my next turn, I lay under the umbrella in the heat of the sun, apparently resting, but in fact willing myself to win. The moment I mentally accepted what appeared to be destiny, the moment I accepted second place, or third, or worse, the competition was over. I knew that no matter what the odds, I must not give in. Muscle is only half of winning; mind is the other half, or possibly three-quarters. But there is a fine line between believing you can win a competition, and putting a medal around your neck before you have won it. The latter leads to over-confidence, cockiness, carelessness — and that is likely to lead to defeat.

Now, as I stepped out of my tracksuit again and walked over to pick the javelin up from the stand for my fourth throw, I knew I had to hold on to my belief in myself. Although I almost had not even come to Rome, although this was definitely the hardest competition I had ever encountered, I had to keep believing I could win. I could not bow under the pressure. I had to go for it.

I had to show everyone — the Smiths who had told me I was a troublemaker and that no one would ever want to adopt me; classmates who had known I was from the home and wouldn't let me forget it; and the woman who had given birth to me but had let me grow up lonely in a children's home. I knew I was a fighter. I had to show that now. When I went out there to throw, no matter how much my arm ached or how frightened I was, I had to, I must, give it my all.

Squinting into the bright light at the people in the stands — there were so many of them there, watching me — I looked for Mum, who was chain-smoking. She gave me the thumbs up sign. Picking up the javelin, holding it loosely in the fingers of my right hand, I walked to the red Tartan run-up to take my fourth throw.

I felt no anger at Petra, none of the aggression at the enemy that can win you through. For Petra I felt only respect. It was a pity we could not both be world champion, but we could not. But if it had to be just one of us, it was, if I had any say in it, going to be me.

Taking a long, deep breath, I let my anger at the past flow out of me like water through a colander. I still used Mum's homely analogy. The green field beyond me where I would throw my javelin was dotted with official markers. It was like any stadium field, but it was the modern Coliseum in Rome, the heir to the most famous stadium in the world, the ancient Colosseum of the history books. And these were the World Championships, aside from the Olympics, the greatest occasion in sport. For a moment, I felt almost too much awe.

Then, becoming aware of every muscle in my body, forgetting the crowd, forgetting the occasion, I thought only of the throw I was about to make. Striding forward with my arm held high, the javelin aloft, but pointing downwards, I felt a rush of determination flow through my veins like a hypodermic of adrenalin. Running now, quickly, surely, I raised the point of the javelin heavenwards, and with a swift, strong whip of my arm forward, bowled it like a molten cricket ball into the sky.

The roar from the crowd, not just the British contingent, soothed the sharp stab of pain I felt in my throwing shoulder. The score-board registered 73.16 metres, a metre and a half further than Petra. I was in the lead. But, as Petra still had three more throws, anything could happen. I bit my lip.

Petra, her blond hair darkened with sweat, tried not to look defeated. She was sure of silver, but she too wanted gold. She picked up the javelin and ran with it, gritting her teeth as she let it go. But her answering 71.56 metre, fourth-round throw did not increase her distance. I was still in the lead.

As I stood on the runway ready to take my fifth throw, I was full of confidence, but my shoulder was throbbing. Petra would have two more chances to increase her distance. I must underline my lead. Concentrating only on the task in hand, I no longer thought of Petra or saw the crowd. Aware only of the javelin, of the turf in the distance and myself, aware only of the feat I had to accomplish, I held the javelin aloft, and began to run. And then I let go. At the precise moment of release, I knew it would be a good throw. The angle of release was right and there had been power in my throw. I watched the javelin soar 76.64 metres into the distance before it landed on the turf. I was elated. It was the third longest throw in history. Only Petra's world record throw and mine, which she had superseded, were further. I now led the competition by nearly 5 metres.

The crowd roared approval. Then it became hushed. Like me the crowd was wondering nervously what Petra's answering throw would be?

With relief, but concern too because her ego would be bruised, I realised her throw was a foul, a no-throw. I was still in the lead. My own final throw was another good one: 72.28 metres. My arm was aching, and when Petra stepped up to take her sixth and last throw of the competition, I held my breath.

Anything could happen. As her throw sailed through the humid air of Rome, I exhaled slowly. It was well short of the 60-metre line. I felt for her, I really did. But then, suddenly, I realised what had happened. Petra would have to be content with silver, as Beate Peters clearly was with bronze. Tessa, throwing her best of the season, 67.54, was out of the medals. I had won! There were tears in my eyes. I had won! I had won Britain's only gold medal at the World Championships. Spontaneously, as before in Stuttgart, I wiggled my hips in happiness, a victory wiggle.

Later that day, at the start of the medals ceremony, as I stood on the grass, arms clasped behind my back, with Petra on one side of me and Beate on the other, I thought of Steve who had died in the Falklands and the song he had said was mine: *Top of the World.* I wished he was here to see it and share my joy and to hear the words that were coming over the loudspeaker: *PRIMA ET CHAMPIONESSE DEL MONDO FATIMA WHITBREAD.*

The crowd gave a loud, friendly roar. It was happening. At last. My face wreathed in smiles, I took one big step on to the white victory platform. Then, as I had been instructed to do, I leaned forward so that the gold medal could be hung by its necklace of ribbon around my neck. The white-haired official who bestowed this honour then gave me the obligatory kiss. Next Petra and after her Beate received their medals and their kisses.

Then, as I stood on the victory platform, gazing at the thousands of cheering people in the stadium and at the foothills of Rome visible beyond, as I waved to my father and brothers and grandparents at home and to the rest of my friends watching on satellite TV, as I thought fleetingly again of Steve's prediction that I would be 'Top of the World', the Olympic orchestra struck up the British National Anthem.

Once again I felt gratitude to Mum, my coach, who had taught me far more than technique. Which is not to knock the technique – I was more than grateful for that too. I felt gratitude too to Andy, my manager, for spurring me on despite that injury. And I felt proud of my achievement, proud for myself, proud for the British people. Just in the nick of time, on the last day we had grabbed a gold medal.

I felt a wonderful, joyful, rare elation.

Instinctively, I put that gold medal, the size of a biscuit, in my mouth and bit on it, hard – to make sure it was real. I wanted too to make sure *I* was real.

The medal was, I was, and my victory was. As I stood there sweating in the sun at the Rome Coliseum, knowing I was number one in the world, *Prima*, I was tired and my arm ached but I had never felt better in my life.

15

Heart and Seoul

The whole nation, I was told, was celebrating my victory. Ecstatic British well-wishers found me even in Rome. Many of them said that by winning our only gold medal, I had saved British pride. I knew that was an exaggeration – British pride may on occasion need boosting but it certainly doesn't need saving.

I couldn't wait to get home.

But when I arrived at Heathrow, the first question I was asked – by the man from *Panorama* – was, do you take drugs? The David Jenkins drugs scandal had just broken. Jenkins, who was British but lived in Los Angeles, had been named as the brains behind a drugs ring that was supplying anabolic steroids all over the United States. British athletes were not even named in the case but to the man from *Panorama*, evidently, anyone was fair game. I felt my homecoming was the wrong moment for the drug question. If I had been a man I would have bopped him one, but as a woman I had to be polite.

I explained yet again that I had been tested five times that year, winter as well as summer. I had even put myself in for a test at a meeting where I wasn't competing, to set an example. And I am not the only one. Not only are British athletes tested at events during the season, but Britain has year-round random testing, and is among the most rigorous testing countries in the world. It is sheer prejudice to think that women can only build muscles with chemical help. It is a notion that comes from the stereotype of the weaker sex. The way I get my muscles is by sweat and hard work. I can bench press 95 kilos, and three times a week I push myself hard to put in the sets and reps I need, as I have been doing,

180

whether I feel like it or not, for a dozen years.

Not long after my homecoming, I was stopped on the M25 for speeding at 108.46 mph. I had a lot on my mind that day. Mum had had a cancerous growth removed from her face, but we didn't know yet how serious the skin cancer actually was. Later that morning I was going to drive her to the doctor to get the results of the laboratory tests. The whole family was frightened. Life without Mum was unthinkable.

There was little traffic on the M25. It was about eleven a.m., the road was dry, and the car, my new Mazda RX7, was powerful. I was on the way back from my osteopath in St Albans where I had gone to get treatment for my still painful shoulder. It was virtually my first drive alone in my new car. Immersed in thoughts about Mum, worried a bit about my injury, and mulling over the honours and the new demands that people were suddenly making on me, I hadn't realised I was going so fast. When I saw the police car parked on the hard shoulder, I glanced down at my speedometer and was amazed. In the rear-view mirror, I saw the police drive out on to the motorway, so I immediately pulled over.

The elder of the two policemen, who must have been near retirement, said that he knew who I was and that I should know better. He was right of course, but when I apologised profusely, and said I hadn't realised I was going so fast, he remained cool and unfriendly. It seemed to me that he was disappointed at not having had to chase me. His partner, a young man, didn't say much. I felt he would have been friendlier if the older officer wasn't standing there, disapproving. I wasn't wearing very much – shorts and a short-sleeved shirt – and the younger man, trying to keep his eyes off me, examined the body of my car quite thoroughly.

At home, I discovered that Mum had gone on her own to get the results early, because she knew how anxious I was. She was going to be all right. I took my driving documents in to my local police station where the officers were very nice. They said that I probably ought to get a solicitor because disqualification was usually recommended for speeding offences of more than 100 mph. A driving ban would make it hard for me to get to training sessions or to the charity functions, fund-raising events and young athletes projects for which I was now much in demand. Obviously, the officials of my sport were worried. So was I.

The case came up on 30 November, and I arrived at Romford Magistrates Court on the outskirts of London at ten a.m. From my point of view, it was not an ideal morning to be in court. The Thames Television sporting awards were being presented at the Savoy Hotel in central London at 12.30 p.m. that day, and I was a contender. Although I wanted to be there badly, I had not requested a change of date for the court hearing because I felt it might annoy the court.

Many of the other defendants waiting in the corridor recognised me. And when it dawned on the court usher that the F. Whitbread on the court list was me, she rushed off to tell the whole staff, who appeared from their various offices to gawk. I felt on display, like a goldfish in a bowl. I hurried into the austere courtroom, where I sat unobtrusively at the back, listening to the cases that preceded mine. I was dressed up for the Thames award ceremony in a new grey suit which I had helped to design, but in court I kept my coat on. When I was called to the front, I stood before the two magistrates, a man and a woman, and pleaded guilty.

The female magistrate who appeared to be in charge listened intently to every word of the proceedings, but she stopped taking notes in the middle of my solicitor's presentation. That made me very anxious. I jumped to the conclusion that she had made up her mind to ban me. Eric Shirley, who is one of the few practical men in athletics, had volunteered to speak in court on my behalf. I was certain that Eric's short, brilliant appeal, explaining how damaging to me as an athlete and to my sport a ban would be, was going to be in vain.

As the two magistrates left the courtroom to decide the penalty, I silently berated myself. I felt as if I was in a no-win situation. If I was banned that would be awkward, and if I wasn't, it would be equally awkward. Certain segments of the media would claim that the courts had shown favouritism. The whole mess was entirely my own fault. I shouldn't have been speeding no matter what.

The best possible outcome, really, was a short ban. To my relief, that is precisely what the magistrates decided. I was fined £120 plus £8 court costs and banned for two weeks. But there was no time to express relief or dismay. I had to hurry to the Savoy.

As I walked quickly across the opulent hotel foyer, the uniformed staff discreetly refrained from staring. When I reached the party, I saw why. I was not that special. The room was full of sporting celebrities – Denis Compton, Derek Underwood, Mike Gatting, Ossie Ardiles, Virginia Leng. The snooker champions Steve Davis and Jimmy White, who had faced each other in Preston just the night before in a match that went to the final frame, were talking intently.

At lunch, I sat next to the popstar David Essex, who was utterly charming. It was stimulating to have a conversation for once that did not involve sport. Richard Branson was also at our table. Gary Mabbutt, the Tottenham footballer joined us. I noticed Tessa at the table behind us, accompanied by an attractive young man who turned out to be her agent from the Adam Faith organisation. ITV's Brian Moore introduced me to David Pleat, who had just parted company with Tottenham Hotspur football club. He seemed in good spirits.

There was a string of awards before the main event, the prestigious Thames Television Panasonic Award. The grand prix driver Jack Brabham, one of the true greats of his sport, read out the four nominees: golf champion Nick Faldo, boxer Frank Bruno, snooker champion Steve Davis, and me. The year before, when I set a world record and won the European Championships, I had been runner up for this award. To my delight, this time I was the winner. I was very pleased.

But what I really wanted, what I had always wanted, was to join the ranks of my heroes and heroines as BBC Television Sports Personality of the Year. Even at the children's home, I had dreamed of it. What makes the BBC award so special is that the viewers choose the recipient, by voting for the winner. Since Rome, I had not been shy about telling people that I yearned for this honour. I am not coy. Why should I pretend to be?

Sitting through the long awards ceremony at BBC Television Centre, I could feel myself becoming more and more nervous. The year before I had been runner-up to Nigel Mansell, the formula one motor-racing driver who had nearly won the world championship. Nearly winning doesn't usually get many votes, but Nigel obviously had won the hearts of many people. I loved the British public, and I needed to know for sure that they also cared about me. I had been proud to be second, ahead of Kenny Dalglish, the Liverpool footballer, and also to finish ahead of all my track and field colleagues, many of whom had had fine years. Some of them were none too pleased either that the first-placed athlete was female. How would they feel if I now actually won the award? I glanced over at Steve Cram who was seated beside me. He immediately smiled. There was not a shred of hostility. In fact, Crammie was rather sweet all evening. I even momentarily considered asking him to change seats with me, because I was seated on the aisle, and my black and white polka dot dress, which was slit to the thigh, was riding up well over my knees. I had had the dress made specially, but now I was a bundle of nerves, and began to worry that as the camera scanned the aisle, the dress would seem too revealing.

Obviously, moving in the middle of the proceedings would be a distraction. I sat tight and listened to the presenter describing Ian Woosnam's exploits on the golf course. Ian had had a superb year, and as every moment was recounted, I became more and more certain that he was going to win. But I knew I had to keep the disappointment from my face. Then Ian Woosnam was awarded third place, and I didn't know whether to feel relief or upset. The viewers had ranked one of the world's top golfers only third. What hope was there for me? Next came the name of the runner-up, none other than the world snooker champion Steve Davis. Again, I felt mixed emotions. It had come to the crunch. If I was going to win anything, it would be the ultimate prize. I held my fingers to my mouth as I waited for the name of the winner, and then at last I heard it, Fatima Whitbread.

The applause was thunderous. I could feel my grin spread literally from ear to ear. If anyone was smiling more than I was, it was Mum. I was overcome with elation. I was stunned. So many people had told me a woman couldn't win. I could barely believe my good fortune.

I was the first woman in ten years to win the most prestigious sporting award in the land. Sport was still a man's world. My most recent female predecessor was none other than Virginia Wade, who won in 1977, after becoming the Wimbledon champion in the year of the Queen's silver jubilee. Her Wimbledon victory had truly been an occasion of national celebration.

Somehow I managed to walk up to accept the award. Thank goodness I was dressed up to the nines. I was amused to hear the commentator say that this was the year of the wiggle. I said a few words that I meant sincerely – thanking every one of the British public, and wishing them all good wishes for the New Year. Please, I added, make a little wish for me too.

Two days later I went to Buckingham Palace to receive an MBE. I had been to the Palace before, for the first time in 1983, to accept the Sybil Abrahams Award from Prince Philip. But now I was going to receive an even higher honour. Months earlier, I had been told that my name was being put forward for an MBE in the Queen's Birthday Honours list. I was so thrilled. Me, Fatima, the girl from the home, on the Queen's Birthday Honours list.

I wrote back immediately accepting the invitation and saying how privileged I felt. The invitation had stressed that the nomination was confidential, and for once I kept a secret to myself, not telling anyone, even my family, the news. When the nominations were at last announced, on the 13 June 1987, I was at Gateshead in the midst of a javelin competition. A message of congratulations was displayed on the electronic scoreboard. I felt very emotional when the crowd in the stadium gave me a tremendous round of applause.

The MBEs are presented at Buckingham Palace in alphabetical order. Since 'W' is the twenty-third letter of the alphabet, it wasn't until the 15 December, two months after the World Championships, that I was to go to the Palace to receive mine from the Queen. I asked my mother and my grandmother to accompany me. We drove swiftly through the morning traffic, but at Canning Town, on the perimeter of the East End, we came practically to a standstill. The flyover was blocked. My blood pressure rose to new heights as I thought I might miss the ceremony. But we eventually found an alternate route through the drab back streets of Stepney and Limehouse, a stark contrast to the elegance that awaited us at Buckingham Palace. After what seemed like hours, we arrived at the Mall with ten minutes to spare and joined the queue of cars.

Security was very strict. A policeman leaned into the car to check that we had invitation cards and the letter of information. Then we were waved along into the Palace's central courtyard, which is not visible to the public. Another policeman checked the boot, looked under the bonnet and even examined the bottom of the car to make sure that there were no weapons or bombs.

When Mum, nan and I walked up to the door of the Palace, our credentials were checked once more, and then we were allowed to enter. Leaving our coats in the cloakroom, we descended a spiral staircase to the plush toilets to freshen up. We had been on the road for over two hours. I was wearing a blue dress, which I had designed myself and had had specially made for the occasion. In the mirror, I saw with relief that the dress had travelled well and was not creased.

Upstairs, where the presentations were to be made, I was captivated by the works of art that were displayed on the walls. Mum and nan were ushered to their seats, and I to mine in the area cordoned off with the other prospective MBEs. We were from all walks of life — and from all over the realm. As we waited, members of the palace staff and many of my fellow recipients came over to congratulate me on my athletics achievements, to shake my hand and to get my autograph. I was very astonished and moved to be regarded as a celebrity in such distinguished company.

Now it was almost time for the ceremony to begin. One of the palace staff attached a small pin to the front of my blue dress. The Queen would use the pin to attach the MBE. The first name was called, then another and another. When at last I heard mine, I walked forward three paces as I had been instructed to do, and turned left to face the Queen. Her Majesty was wearing a very elegant yellow outfit. I curtsied.

Her Majesty said that she was delighted to meet me, and that she had watched me receive the BBC Sports Personality of the Year award on television two nights before. I told her that to receive the MBE was the completion of a wonderful year.

Her Majesty attached the MBE to my dress, and then she shook my hand. I curtsied once more. On the way back to my seat, I caught a glimpse of Mum and nan beaming. I felt elated and a little solemn. This was one of the great honours of the land, one of the highest honours I would ever receive. I savoured the moment.

When the band struck up the national anthem, memories of the gold medal ceremonies at the European Championships in Stuttgart and at the Worlds in Rome came flooding back to me, making me proud to be British. Her Majesty departed, and then there was a gentle, excited mêlée as the hugging and kissing and congratulating by relatives and friends began.

Leaving the hall in high spirits, as I passed one of the ceremonial guards who was standing to attention holding his sword, I said lightly, 'You look very smart even though there is a large speck of dust on your sword.'

The guardsman remained standing to attention, but he couldn't help smiling just a little.

Then a journalist, who turned out to be from LBC Radio, pushed forward. Shoving a microphone under my nose, he asked me how I felt about drugs in athletics. I was shocked at the tastelessness of the question, given the moment, and I said so. Here I was leaving Buckingham Palace after a touching occasion and I was faced with a replay of my tarnished Heathrow homecoming. I could well understand why some of my colleagues in sport had reacted strongly to reporters in the past.

Nevertheless, I maintained my composure, and answered the question. Sport is a continuation of society and has the ills of society, so there is bound to be drug abuse by a minority of athletes around the world. My comment that the question had been in poor taste was omitted when the interview was broadcast.

Outside the Palace the sun was shining brightly. In the court-yard, I held up my MBE for the television and newspaper cameras. I signed some autographs, and then we drove across the area where the changing of the guard had just occurred, and out of Buckingham Palace. Mum and nan, one on either side, had linked arms with me. As we drove down the Mall towards Trafalgar Square I felt so proud.

We stopped for lunch at the Tower Hotel. Then it was immediately back to training. I drove my Mazda RX7 to the weight-training shed where I put in the session I normally would have done first thing in the morning. Then I went to Blackshots playing-field for a session of strenuous bounding. As I drove home along the A13, I noticed a man walking along the road carrying an air rifle. Suddenly, he turned and shot at me, shattering the windscreen.

I didn't stop. Once home, I alerted the police, but I didn't give my name because I didn't want the media to hear of the incident. Some of them would have let their imaginations run down ugly corridors. I didn't want them camping on my doorstep either, asking how I felt when the bullet struck, and what it had to do with my MBE.

Even though I knew that the bullet had been fired at me only by the merest chance, I was a little shaken. All in all, it had been quite a day. But I was not going to let a moment of random viciousness poison my memories of the day I met the Queen.

Nor will I ever forget the day I went to Number Ten to have cocktails with Mrs Thatcher. As soon as I arrived, all semblance of nerves disappeared because I saw so many familiar faces from the world of sport. Golfers Nick Faldo, Tony Jacklin and Ken Brown were there with their spouses; as was Nigel Mansell. But I didn't mind a bit that I was on my own. Everyone was very chatty, and I felt terrific in the conservative royal blue outfit I had on. It was another of those I had designed myself.

Mrs Thatcher was wearing blue too, a darker shade than mine. As ever, she seemed very cool and in complete control of the situation. Her husband Denis was standing beside her. She welcomed me and told me to make myself at home. Peeking into the cabinet room, I could sense almost palpably the power the room had. So many decisions which had changed the world had been made here. So many more would be in the future.

I munched a few sandwiches and talked to Colin Cowdrey, the

former England cricket captain, of whom I am a fan. Then one typical 'pain-in-the-neck' – and there is always one at these functions – tried to corner me. He went on about how important you had to be to get an invitation and therefore how important he was. I was rescued by a member of the prime minister's staff asking me to join Mrs Thatcher for photographs.

I had almost reached the prime minister when I was waylaid by another guest. Mrs Thatcher herself then stepped in and took me aside for the photo session. There were a number of pictures taken and the one of me and Nigel Mansell with the prime minister eventually appeared in the press.

When we had completed the photos and were well out of the prime minister's earshot, Nigel said wryly that he was pleased to have been photographed with the two most powerful women in Britain.

'I hope you don't mean brain and brawn.'

'That is not at all the situation,' he said.

We had a good laugh.

But my shoes were hurting my feet. I found a little room off the main one, and wriggled out of them. Sitting there in my stocking feet, surrounded by history but very much at ease, I had a chat with one of Mrs Thatcher's staff about the pressures that are placed on a prime minister and those that are placed on a world champion. Hers, as you can imagine, made my pressures pale into insignificance. That talk was, I realised instantly, good for me. As I was leaving I was introduced to Willie Whitelaw. By now Mrs Thatcher was engaged with her advisers. I thanked Denis Thatcher for his hospitality and extended my gratitude through him to his wife.

The new year began with a training injury, first it affected my hamstring, then my heel. Javelin throwers are rarely fully fit – I was used to pain. But very soon 1988 began to turn into a nightmare. My shoulder was tender, and I began to feel a tiredness I could not shake off. That lassitude, that lack of vigour, depressed me far more than the pain. But when I started the phase of my winter training that requires run-ups, the pain in my foot was so intense I literally collapsed, unable to put any weight at all on the foot. Unfortunately, the fact that a small bone in my foot was very slightly out of place had gone unnoticed for much of the winter. As the muscles began to tighten around the bone, they too were slightly out of place, causing intense pain when I used my foot.

And I still had none of my usual energy and high spirits. There were no jokes cracked during training anymore in Chadwell St Mary. I felt down in the dumps. Even at the unveiling of my likeness in wax at Madame Tussaud's, I felt way under par, although I had posed for the waxwork and was proud to be the only British athlete other than Daley Thompson whose image stands in the prestigious Hall of Greats. John McEnroe had been removed to make room for me. But nothing gave me much of a lift. I felt like an ailing old woman, instead of the world champion I was.

After a series of tests, the doctor diagnosed glandular fever. How unlucky. This was the Olympic year; I wanted so desperately to be fit. I kept pushing myself. I had to try to take it in my stride. Continuing to train would pose no danger, the doctor said, but I might find it rather difficult.

How right he was. Some days I couldn't even get out of bed. It was so frustrating, so ironic. I had been training for more than a dozen years to be ready for these Olympic games, and now my strength, my power, seemed to be deserting me. My head would be blazing with fever, but I felt there was no time to rest. Pushing myself so hard I became even more run-down. I collapsed during a training session. Then, towards the end of June, I succumbed to another infection, a nasty abcess which had to be surgically removed from a rather undignified part of my anatomy, my bum.

On the TV above my hospital bed, I watched Martina Navratilova defeat Chrissie Evert in a spell-binding Wimbledon match, and then I watched Steffi Graf wreak Chrissie's revenge on Martina in the final. Steffi is a champion's champion, but so too is Martina, and I felt some sorrow that she did not attain the record number of Wimbledon titles that she so wanted.

The next day I came out of hospital and began the task of rebuilding myself, starting my season's training again almost at the beginning. I was at least two months behind schedule. I would give it everything I had, and I had my years of dedicated training to call on, like muscle in the bank. It had even been earning interest, computed in skill, self-confidence and strength. But I knew too that athletics was in a period of muscular inflation. My fear was that one terrible season might cost me everything at the Games.

Meanwhile Petra Felke was throwing her javelin brilliantly all over Europe. For me, the Olympic odds were getting worse and worse. Many people suggested it was too late, and that I should call it a day. I did not want to go to Seoul and disgrace myself, but equally, I knew I could never ever respect myself if I gave up while there was still a chance, no matter how small, that I could be fit enough to win a medal.

In mid-August, after six weeks off, I competed at Gateshead in the Dairy Crest Games. With no one there of note to throw against, it was less a competition than a public training session. I had to work at making the adrenalin flow. My shoulder still hurt, but I won. It was good to be back. In Brussels and Zurich I faced stiffer competition, and was victorious. That reminded me how much I like winning. Three weeks before the Games I had my last hard competition, at Crystal Palace against Tessa. I won with 69.40.

My shoulder had been flaring up after every training session and every competition, but it was slowly getting stronger. I was throwing further every day. Although I had not achieved my previous standard, and I was living in constant pain, I felt I was in with a chance at the Olympics, even when Petra, who had returned with the East German team from altitude training in Mexico, shattered the world record. I reassured myself with the thought that only the year before Petra had broken the world record shortly before the World Championships at Rome and none the less I had beaten her for gold.

As I got on the plane for the long journey to Seoul, I felt full of hope. No one could possibly want to win as much as I did. In world-class competition, you call on all the resources of your body, and the will to win is tremendously important.

It was pleasantly hot in Seoul. After our chill summer, you

couldn't fault the weather, but Seoul was, many people thought, a strange place to stage the Olympics. It was a centre of political turmoil. Riots in the city had been front page news for months. North Korea which had been refused the right to join South Korea in hosting the Games, threatened to disrupt them. With the border between North and South Korea just 35 miles north of Seoul, an artillery shell lobbed at the stadium from north of the border would hit its mark. There was a lot of talk, but it was pointless to imagine dire possibilities. There was nothing I could do to prevent trouble. I could only hope that those in charge were acting responsibly. My own responsibility surely was to focus on the task before me, and to do my best, no matter what. Even after the Games had started, there were riots just 15 miles from the stadium, between the radical students who threw fire bombs and stones, and the police, who responded with violence and tear gas.

The Olympic village, of course, was well insulated from disturbances, but Dad had been worried about Mum who was staying in the city at the Seoul Plaza Hotel, where I joined her as often as I could. Neither of us got a whiff of tear gas, thank goodness. In the days before my event, I spent my time training in the big throwing field near the Han river, chatting with friends from all over the world, including Petra Felke, and trying to avoid queuing – even for breakfast at the Olympic village you had to wait for forty minutes. Every day I got treatment from the Belgian physiotherapist for my throbbing shoulder.

Whenever I could, I got well away from the stark, new, modern Olympic complex and stood in the quiet serenity of the gardens beneath the ancient monument called the Namdaemum. It was a place to meditate, to feel quiet inside. On the way back to the Olympic hubbub, I looked for the wizened old woman with smiling eyes who sold chestnuts for 1,000 Wong.

At last, on 25 September, came the javelin qualifying round. Tessa failed utterly to qualify for the final. So did Tiina Lillak, the long, lanky, talented, former world champion from Finland. Lillak's failure was a shock. On the other hand, Petra Felke, East Germany's best hope, was on top form. She qualified easily on her first throw. Now it was down to me.

With dismay I saw my first throw land short of the 63 metres qualifying standard, and felt a stab of pain in my shoulder. I was just a little shaken, I told myself, because during the warm-up at the Han, a Chinese thrower's javelin had skidded crazily along the ground, nearly jabbing me. I threw again and watched my second throw also peter out. Usually, even at the worst of times I can throw 63 metres. I had to pull myself together – now – or it would be a return of the depressing Moscow Olympics eight years ago where Tessa and I both failed to qualify. For me that had been only a hiccup, since I had mainly gone to Moscow to gain experience. But now I was in my prime.

You get six throws in the final, but only three in the qualifying round. This was my last chance. I couldn't let myself and Britain down. Silently, I told myself, you can't afford self-doubt, Fatima. It's too pricey. You will throw the qualifying standard, and 5 bloody metres more. You can do it. *I can do it.* And I did, qualifying on my last throw with 68.44 metres, the best throw of the day. Things were looking up.

Meanwhile, in London, I was the centre of a tempest in the tabloids. The *Daily Mail* had reported in a serialisation from this book that as a girl I was raped. Two days later the *Sun* printed a front-page story and the photograph of a man who denied raping me. What was extremely odd about this was that the man has never been accused, not in the *Daily Mail* and not in this book. If I ever knew it, I do not remember the name of the man who raped me. And I knew too little about the housekeeping arrangements of the woman who said she was my mother to know if he lived with her on a long-term basis or was just 'visiting'. On the day before I was to compete in the Olympic final, the *News of the World* got in on the act. The woman was quoted as saying of me, 'I'm praying she loses.'

But in Seoul that night, the night before the final, I knew nothing of all this. The British officials had skilfully protected me from the press. Mum did not tell me that the man from the *News of the World* had been quite rude to her. During our evening meal at the Seoul Hilton the only thing I was apprehensive about was the looming final late the next afternoon. I was so anxious that I didn't eat as much as I have been known to.

I didn't say as much as usual either, just sat there listening vaguely to the background music, a pleasant medley. I perked up though when the band began to play *We've Only Just Begun*, the song Steve used to sing to me. Recognising the song, Mum grinned at me and said, 'This is an omen.'

The Olympic stadium was deeply impressive. It was bold, modern architecture, usually framed by a blue sky. As I picked up my javelin and went out to throw, I felt a proper sense of occasion, but I was in no way intimidated. That was entirely impossible with a lively British contingent of fans seated right behind the javelin run-up, cheering my every move. I gave them a big smile, and then after noting that the sky had become cloudy, I became oblivious to everything but the competition, which began with a flourish.

Petra, on her first throw, threw further than 70 metres, breaking the Olympic record. My first throw was rubbish. On her second throw, Petra, who is two years my senior and was in the midst of her best season ever, increased her distance to an astonishing 74.68 metres. Well, no matter, I was still going for gold. Self-doubt was a luxury I could not afford. I shut off from it and from the stabbing pain of my shoulder, and with a yell I threw 67.46, which put me in the silver medal position.

I wanted a 70-metre throw. Badly. But the magic seemed to have gone out of Seoul stadium. The breeze was now unpredictable. Petra's next two throws were on average worse than mine, and the new East German, 21-year-old Beate Koch, seemed unable to surpass me. On the penultimate throw, I increased my distance slightly, and then came the sixth throw, my last opportunity.

Wrapping my mind round the javelin, visualising the perfect shot, one in which every muscle was instructed correctly and did as it was told, regardless of whether it hurt or not, I held the javelin aloft and began to run. Then, with a loud shout, I whipped my arm forward, and let the javelin go. I could feel it was a good throw, not my best, but a good one. Would it be good enough?

The javelin rose high. I held my breath. Where would it land? Would it be far enough? My shoulder was throbbing. I kept my mind entirely on the flight of the javelin, willing it to go further, even further. Please, I muttered. Please. And the javelin continued to soar. Right, I said, javelin, you just take your time. After what seemed a millennium, it nosed towards the ground, landing gracefully at 70.32 metres, my longest throw of the season. I couldn't ask for more than that. After a year of illness and injury, I had won a silver medal at the Olympics. I had gone for gold but it wasn't to be. That's sport. That's life. I wasn't disappointed because it had been such a struggle all the way even to throw at Seoul. I hoped no one at home was disappointed. A silver medal is no mean achievement. I had won my silver with a throw that beat the old Olympic record, which I was pleased about because it meant I had beaten my old adversary Tessa's record.

And all credit to Petra Felke, who had beaten me. Petra is a great thrower. When I won gold at the European Championships, she had to put up with silver. When I won gold at the World Championships, she got silver again. Between us we have thrown some incredible distances and put the women's javelin on the world sporting map. She has been competing for sixteen years, and I am glad she has finally won a major title. I'm only sorry it had to be this one.

Now that the Games were over I was looking forward to some quiet times. Shortly before Seoul, I had moved into an eighteenth-century cottage, not too far away from the family. The cottage, with its crushed raspberry carpeting and, in the lounge, a chandelier with fifteen glittering lights, is my dream house, where I intend to cook many, many lavish meals for Mum, Dad, my two brothers, grandad and nan, and other special people. We will eat a lot and laugh a lot and feel close. My nosey dog Champ will no doubt butt in. But all that, of course, will have to fit in between javelin training sessions. Javelin throwers mature like wine, and I still want the Olympic title. At the Games in Los Angeles I won bronze. In Seoul, it was silver. In Barcelona in 1992, it has to be gold.

Olivier

ANTHONY HOLDEN

'The most complete book about Olivier . . . benefits from the quality of the writing and the thoroughness of the research. Light, bright, incisive'
INDEPENDENT

'The most eagerly awaited and the most monumental study of the Great Man yet mounted . . . sharp, unsentimental, up-to-date and fully worthy of its chameleonesque figure'
TIME OUT

'An important biographer and a major subject. A substantial achievement'
SUNDAY TIMES

'What we want from a good showbiz biography is gossip, information and intelligent star-struck prose, and Holden provides it all . . . this thoroughly researched and indefatigable biography often seems to be the history of the English theatre in this century'
THE STAGE

0 7221 4857 7   BIOGRAPHY   £5.99